GRAB YOUR TICKET AND YOUR SUITCASE

Dan French

DAN FRENCH

Front cover photo: Jim's suitcase by Jim Page
End photo: Dan in 2008 by Jim Page

Photos other than mine credited where known

Cover design by Dave Percival

'Grab your ticket and your suitcase'
from 'Land Of Hope And Dreams'
by Bruce Springsteen

Slane 1985 story by Mike Saunders

Published 2025

ISBN: 978-1-7385743-5-3

TRETHEWEY

tretheweypress@gmail.com

GRAB YOUR

TICKET

AND YOUR SUITCASE

A personal Bruce Springsteen concert history

Dan French

INTRODUCTION

I first saw Bruce Springsteen in concert in 1981, the first of many times - and having always collected all my show ticket stubs where possible, it seems a natural way to reflect on my own diary of the concerts through the ticket stubs. Concert tickets have evolved over the years, and while most of these are from the era of paper tickets, many current e-tickets only exist in digital formats, and are not designed to be collected as stubs unless you save the image somehow, as I still aim to do. The change in ticket design is also encompassed here.

Ticket stubs can serve as markers in the life of a fan; not just souvenirs of concerts, but also milestones for celebrating friends, family, travel, experiences and moments in history.

Some tickets have more of a story attached to them than others, such as my first experience in Frankfurt, or the birthday weekend at Slane Castle in 1985; but I value them all, and hope readers also enjoy the cultural time travel they offer, whether you were at similar shows or not.

Many thanks follow, and I especially need to highlight my gratitude to the Brucebase site and its curator Danny for invaluable reference information needed for these stories; and fellow show-going aficionado Mike with his excellent memory for details, vigilance, proofreading, Druidic navigation and all-round good company along the road.

As the man sang: ‘Grab your ticket and your suitcase…’

Dan French
2025
tretheweypress@gmail.com

ROLL CALL! BIG THANKS ...

The Shipmates and Geezers in Glasses: Mike, Dave, Jim, Neil and Gordon, Jeff - and Gill, Jayne, Pamela and Julie

The It'd Be Rude Not To Crew (Bruce gang) & co: Linda, Helen, Magda, Sue, Sharon, John W, Caroline & Ralph, Yvonne, Annie & Peter, Brenda & Chris, Ward & Thessa, Jacco & Jeanne, Sergio & Franca, Astrid, Carolyn, Kim, Keith, Will, Fros & Michael

E Street Fam: Janice, Salla, Laura, Paul, Molly, Saoirse

The Teddy Bears: Peter (and the PHL), Arf (and Janice H), John W (again), and Graham

Neil F; Rena, Ilona & Hubert; Mats; Mikey H; Greg T; Geoff N; Glen P; Nicki G, Mark R and Tom M; Deirdre; Ekaterina ('Kate'), Tanya and Luba; Alan, Paul and Paul; Ken L; Jay F; Anne M and Dari; Ellinor, Annsofie, Anna & Oliver, Anne S, Soren and Jennifer; Erik; Deborah M; Jon P; Jayne; 'Uncle' John H; Rod; Philip & Cinzia; Paul, Carol & Jack; Matthew; Walter; Simon; Sabine & Ken; Ralf, Margrit and Lisa; Dan-Erik, Glenn and 'The Swedes From Sweden'; Jean-Francois; Marion M; Chantal; Tom C & Rich R; René & Reinie; Harry 'Sole Driver' & Gill, Mike W; Vince, Neil K, Jackie; Lauren V & Barbara; Roger G; Guido; Nick C; Jon C; Alex M; Paul T; Greg & Moira; Mukul; Salvador, Winni & Sarah; Sammy, Annette, Mel, Graham R, Robin, Cam, Julie Y, Bill D, Jenny and Duncan, Anne C, Justin; David B; Beverly and José; Pam S; Tony F and Kevin P; Norma, Mick & Rita; Debs; Carol M; John M & Sylvia; Tom W & Laura; Patrick; Joe F; Donna; Eddy; Lorenzo; Jeremy B; Gary H; 'Max' S; 'Miami' Ronnie C; Clive M; Mike Z; Matt; Martin S; Scott; Malcolm & Brenda; John & Rob; Jan & Jane; Ermanno, Rinaldo; Magnus; Christy; Sebla & Steve; Barry & Nancy; Liz; Flynn, Claudine, Hal; Debra; Lauren; Bernie R; Jeff M, Linda R, Stephanie & Peter, Franky, Thomas, Nicholas and John N (FMT); René S; Julie,

Anita & Paul; Christina; Gordon M; Gillian; Robert; Karen; Billy S & Stephen B; Steven 'Checkered Shirt Guy'; Joanne; Emily; Our Love Is Real; Bobby C; Dick W; Frank S; Barry S; Warren Z; Pete H; Hywel R; Eileen C; Craig S; Ken R; Maggie P; Jesse J; Stan & Jean; Anders; Patti M; Jonathan & Anneli; Ellie & Hope; Peter & Margaret; Ramona; Ruth & Tim; Sindy; Mike S; John C; Ceinwen & Hywel; Vivian; Meena; Victoria & Bruce; Kayleigh; Matty; Mike C; Helen J; María; Paul at The E Street Café; Danny at Brucebase

Ticket Stub Club members and 'Point Blank' readers

The 'Slane Survivors' all

Kezia (concert 'widow' at my shows from 1999 – 2014)

… and of course
Bruce Springsteen and The E Street Band
The (Seeger) Sessions Band
'The Other Band / 1992-1993 Touring Band'

Dedicated to the memory of 'sweet souls departed':

Holly, Mary, Vera, Mandy, Alex, Chris, Steve, Ellen, Judith, Trish, Charles, Connor, Bel, Bernie, Ted (RIP all)

Holly with Bruce
E Street plane 2003

Holly, Thugsgiving 2017
Photo thanks to Molly

CONTENTS

1981

The *River* tour

14 April 1981: Frankfurt, Festhalle

Let me set the scene: when Bruce Springsteen & the E Street Band toured Europe in the spring of 1981 to support their album 'The River', I was living in London, out of work, with only my home-made fanzine 'Point Blank' to my name – I had time on my hands, but I was broke. If I wanted to travel, I hitch-hiked to most places, and slept on friends' floors and sofas. Selling a few fanzines meant I could buy basic necessities to live on, or occasionally stretch to the luxury of a train ticket, and in a few months had already brought me some good friends and many pen-pals I'd never met. When the UK tour was postponed by a couple of months, meaning that the European leg started on the continent rather than in

Britain, I thought I'd have to wait for my first Bruce Springsteen concert. I was wrong…

After the months from December 1980 to March 1981 spent collecting tickets for the UK shows and the postponement announcement, I got a letter from my German pen-pal Rena one day in March with a note saying: see you at the Canadian Pacific Hotel, Frankfurt, 13th April. Enclosed was a side balcony ticket for Frankfurt Festhalle, 14th April (This was upgraded to the 14th row stalls ticket featured here).

My friend John H had been promised a ticket for one of the Paris shows and was going to stay with a friend there. I arranged to meet him in Paris at Easter, and went there first to try and get tickets for various friends in advance. Having been tipped off as to the expected date and place of sale of the Paris tickets, I hitched there only to find no trace of any tickets at the box office or supposed venue. The only indication that Bruce was coming to Europe at all was a window display of singles and posters in a Metro subway: 'Bruce Springsteen en France'! But I was told that the tickets had all been sold before I even arrived (like the early sale at the Edinburgh queue!). Disheartened at the thought of disappointing my friends hoping for tickets, I splashed out on a train from Paris to Frankfurt (I gave up hitching after hours wasted trying to hitch out of Paris) and arrived late on the 13th. Tired and bleary, I was overjoyed to see the huge red sign outside the Festhalle: 'Bruce Springsteen & The E Street Band, 14th April.' At last!

Across the street was the Canadian Pacific hotel: huge, modern and expensive. A self-conscious tramp, I asked at the reception for Rena. A phone call to her room showed she was out, so I left a note for her: gone to sleep in the park (couldn't afford a room!).

Meanwhile…just around the corner from the reception lobby, Rena was waiting for me in the bar, sitting with copies of my fanzine Point Blank displayed (Mike H sent her a bunch for me, marked 'For Display' to get through his office franking machine – Rena, having no explanation – I didn't know! – duly obeyed instructions and displayed them!). Who should wander into the bar but the whole E Street Band, who just happened to be staying in the same luxury hotel, and wanted to buy Max a drink for his birthday! Clarence sees Rena alone, and being the gent he is, sits down with her, puts his arm around her and booms: 'Hey, little girl, are you married?' And there's Rena, sitting between CC and Bruce, surrounded by the band, celebrating! And here's yours truly huddled up in his sleeping bag under a tree near an ornamental lake!

Several drinks later, Rena finds my note, and says to Clarence: 'Hey, we've got to go and find Dan in the park.' So they rush round the park, looking for me, shouting 'Dan French come out tonight!' (I have nothing to hide!) Guess who slept through it all?!

9 am, 14th April: Even more dazed and bleary, I call Rena again and go up to her room and meet her for the first time. 'Dan! Come on, we have to go and wake Clarence.' Uh-huh. Clarence? Clarence. CLARENCE? CLARENCE!! Can it be? Are they here?? Another door: she knocks, and eventually a deep, sleepy voice answers. It's dark inside. There's a huge black guy gripping my hand warmly, and it's him! I'm speechless – knees probably shaking! Clarence has a terrible hangover and can't face the daylight yet. 'I had such a baaad dream, baby' he moans, 'thanks for waking me.' More handshakes, and he flops on the bed. We go and have breakfast in the hotel, spotting Max and various crew-types around. I begin to wake up and realise what's happening!

After a leisurely morning we go back to CC's room to wake him again at midday – knocking first on a door marked 'Do Not Disturb' which Rena calls at: 'Bruce. Bruce?' No reply. Clarence is as glad to see us as if we'd been long-departed friends, but is still not fully awake: let him sleep a little longer, OK? About 2 o'clock, he finally gets up on our 3rd visit and slowly gets washed and dressed. Larger than life and twice as natural! What a start to the day of my first show. Just the start…!

Around 4 or 5 o'clock, after leaving Clarence with Glen P, his personal manager, to sort out his clothes for the show, we wait in the lobby with some American roadies discussing a shopping list of cameras (CC wants an automatic one for holiday snaps). A girl from CBS Germany is checking details on a clipboard. Rena points out Barbara Carr: 'That's Jon Landau's assistant'. I immediately mistake her for Rhoda, Neil G's prime contact, who also works for Landau, and tell Rena I'd heard she (Rhoda) was supposed to have sent me a show review, on Neil's request, for the mag. 'I must introduce you,' insists Rena, and reluctantly I shake hands with a bewildered Barbara Carr as I tell her I'm afraid I never received her review, and that Neil said hi! She must have thought I was crazy!

Gradually, the whole band filters into the lobby, with various girlfriends and wives and crew (no Joyce, as far as I know) and Jon Landau. 'There he is,' says Rena, pointing. Who? That guy with dark glasses and a leather jacket over his shoulder? It's Bruce. I had to look twice to make sure. They all stand near the exit, waiting for the King. Clarence makes his grand entrance at last, and they're ready to go to the soundcheck. Rena and I walk out with CC and the band to where a minibus is waiting. No, let's walk, they say: it's just over the road (you can see the red sign). On the way I'm within a couple of feet of Bruce as we climb over some security fencing (like hurdles) near the entrance. Bruce jumps over one and drops his jacket, which I pick up and pass to him, saying: 'Able to leap tall buildings at a single bound'. 'Right,' he mutters, seeming pre-occupied – thinking of the soundcheck, no doubt. We come to the security limit and Clarence takes us both in with him and the band.

Inside, the Festhalle seems huge: only 4,000 seats? Two balconies, and a figure-8 shaped plan. Glen tells us: 'You'd better have these. Stop you getting questioned.' Two backstage passes. 'You two got tickets?' Yes – here. 'Have these instead'. Row 14, stalls. Hey, thanks, Glen! 'You're welcome. Keep off the stage now'. And while Bruce walks around the hall, the band is on stage and Roy begins a crystal clear intro to 'Hungry Heart' – loud and sparkling. Sounds perfect already! Rena takes photos, despite being told not to.

I sit front row centre in the empty seats to watch and listen to the soundcheck, hardly believing what's happening. An awkward moment when a merchandise guy tells me to stop giving away those magazines, since he fears it might affect his programme sales. I'm too happy to argue. Who cares? They're all playing now apart from Bruce, still circling the balconies with Bruce Jackson. 'Prove It All Night', and Bruce joins the band at last on guitar and then vocals – lazy and serious-faced, but magnificent – effortless, in his element. After one and a half to two hours he's satisfied with those two songs and it's back to the dressing-rooms until showtime: the kids are building up outside, and the armed police look alarming. Harry Sandler, road manager, gives the band Dutch editions of 'The River' album. 'Fainter blue sleeve,' I remark to Roy over his shoulder. Yes, he nods.

We're in Clarence's room with him and Glen when Bruce, tense with hunched shoulders, wanders in. I get up to offer him the seat, when Glen waves us both out: Bruce wants to talk to the Big Man. Time for us to find our seats. Hey, there's Mike H, over on the Mead Gould coach trip! And a few other familiar faces. Lots of American GIs (a base nearby). The excitement is electric! From a hum to a buzz and then a roar as the lights go down. Talk about an adrenalin rush – we're up and on our chairs before we know it. Out of the noise drones the organ whine of 'Factory', and this is it! It's really happening, like living a dream. I don't know if the show was a good one or not – I didn't care – nothing could go wrong! I scribbled the initials of the songs down and yelled myself hoarse and dry.

After the lights went on, Rena and I went backstage: I took a couple of programmes and a badge (from Mike, Kev, and a girl). Exhausted, elated and parched, we waited for at least an hour in a room outside the dressing-room area. There was no drink or food to be had! Various people were there waiting for Bruce, including a German reporter who interviewed Jon Landau while we were all waiting. Landau stressed: no tape interviews. After an age Bruce wandered out, leather jacketed and hair slicked back, grinning and looking fresher than before the show! He greeted friends and well-wishers, and spoke to a reporter briefly. At last he turned, about to go, and walked up to us. He looked at Rena and me, I grabbed my moment and stuck out my hand: 'Hi, Bruce!' Rena said: 'This is the guy who does the magazine.' 'Oh yeah? Where are you from?' London, I said, feeling dumb. Then I remembered the souvenirs, and asked: 'Could you sign these (programmes) for a couple of friends waiting outside?' 'Sure.' He signs the poster centrefolds: 'Who's this for?' 'For Mike.' I gave him a Point Blank leaflet – all the paper I had on me. 'And this is for me – Dan.' He wrote: 'To Dan – thanks for your support. Say hello to everyone for me, Bruce.' Then I gave him the badge: 'Some girl wanted you to have this.' (Bruce is holding the badge in the photo Rena took of us.) He shook hands again and waved goodbye with a smile. 'I'll see you in Britain, if not before!' I called, as he left. Bruce nodded and was gone, hungry but willing to sign more autographs for a group of fans outside. Rena and I left him to it after I'd returned the programmes to Mike and Kev and said goodbye, and we went back to the hotel.

Backstage at Frankfurt – photo thanks to Rena Huerttlen

The next morning we had a late breakfast and left – but not before I encountered Roy by the hotel postcards stand and asked him for a scribble. 'Sure,' he smiled. 'Take it easy.' No-one else was there. (To be continued at Munich…)

16 April 1981: Munich, Olympiahalle

Following the 14 April concert at Frankfurt, we took a train back to Rena's place in Mannheim, and I met Ilona and Hubert, her neighbours. Spent the day resting, and the next day went into town to eat and visit her friend's hi-fi shop. In the afternoon Rena called some hotels in Munich until she found the one Clarence was staying in, the Hilton, and asked him if she and three friends could come to the show tonight. Sure, said the Big Man: ask Glen for your tickets when you come. So Hubert drove Ilona, Rena and I the 200km to Munich that evening! We got to the Olympiahalle just before 8 o'clock, and found Glen – but only three tickets and passes. A misunderstanding: Glen found another set, and we went in.

There was quite a different feel from the Frankfurt atmosphere – moody. Early into the show the crowd surged into a space near the front and Bruce had to stop before introducing 'Independence Day' and ask people to go back to their seats. Rena and I moved from our places in the guest rows on the side down into the stalls where there was room to stand and dance.

Champagne and a Walkman listening session with Clarence and Rena, after the show in his Munich Hilton hotel room – photos thanks to Ilona & Hubert, Rena's Mannheim neighbours and our drivers

As it was the last night in Germany, there was a big reception laid on backstage, and as guests we took the chance to eat and spot Roy, Max, Danny, Garry and Clarence mingling. Bruce and Steve didn't show up this time: we spent a while hunting for the dressing-rooms in the large backstage area, but no luck. So we drove to CC's hotel, went up to his room, and he welcomed us all with champagne! We sat and listened on an unfamiliar new gadget, a Sony Walkman, to his latest recordings on Gary 'US' Bonds' yet to be released 'Dedication': 'That's me!' he'd say, on a sax solo. His other cassettes included the Fabulous Thunderbirds and Stevie Wonder. Rena took photos and got Ilona and Hubert to take some of us. I saw the tour handbook and made a mental note that a second Stafford gig had been pencilled in for 21st May. Entries included: 'Tuesday – day off – have a good time!'

We must have stayed a couple of hours. Clarence offered to give us rooms at the Hilton, but the others had to go to work the next day, so we all drove back in the wee wee hours and left CC to travel to Paris the next day with the band.

(To be continued at Paris...)

18 April 1981: Paris, Palais Des Sports St-Ouen

Continued from Munich…

It was light when Rena and I got back to her place at Mannheim, and I slept until the afternoon. We had a bite to eat, played some records and watched a few German videos – she had a good collection. Rena couldn't go to Paris, so I left and tried to hitch out of Mannheim on the outskirts of town, but gave up after trying for a long time and getting cold and restless. So I took a train again back to Paris, and slept rough once more – Good Friday, I think it was.

On the 18th, I found the address where John H was staying before seeing the show that night, and once again feeling very consciously the tramp, called in at the posh block of apartments, and found him and the friend whose flat it was. It was a relief to speak English to a familiar face and sit on the sunny balcony having coffee! We agreed that although I didn't have a ticket, we'd wander up to the hall, the Palais de Sports on the north side of town, and have a look around. We walked from the Metro stop over the bridge of the river to the site of the odd-shaped sports hall rising on the far banks.

No sign of any posters or ads for the show, but we walked up the drive as far as we could and found a small box-office. It was open, and inside at a table, a little old lady was opening envelopes containing tickets for both shows!

Quickly I borrowed some money from John (which was to take me six months to repay!) and we bought three extra tickets for each show, plus one for John for the Sunday night; we knew that Geoff N and Kristina V were coming and didn't have tickets. We couldn't believe our luck! I was going to see Bruce twice more before I had to go back! It was still early afternoon, so I went and tried to find a call box to phone Neil F in London and tell him that if he could make it over for the Sunday, we'd get him a ticket! But most of the shops with phones were shut, and I only had a little change in coins. We decided to sit tight and wait for Geoff and Kristina, who we met soon after, but first we bumped into Martin E and Marianne! A complete surprise. They had tickets just for the first night and couldn't afford to see both shows. Somehow Geoff or Kristina had got a spare couple, which John sold to a fan – a small queue was building up in the late afternoon, trickling in from town across the bridge.

Unsure whether our tickets were for good seats, as there was no seating plan anywhere, we queued quite near the front of the line as the sun went down. Around 5 o'clock, as expected, a couple of vans came up the drive past us, greeted by cheers and waving when the crowd spotted the passengers. They had to drive slowly up the narrow road which we were partly blocking, and I had a good view of a smiling Clarence and Bruce in one of the vans. They waved in our direction, and I'm sure Bruce's face showed an expression of recognition as I looked at him! And then they were through the gates and into the hall for the soundcheck. Soon we heard the now familiar booming echo of 'Hungry Heart' and 'Prove It All Night'. It was too far from their centre-of-town hotel for the band to go back before the show, and around 7 o'clock they opened the gates and we filed in, looking at the hall, and a few of us tried the outrageously priced drinks and snacks. To the right and back of the stalls (unfixed chairs) were steps, like an amphitheatre, and large windows to the right. Although they drew curtains over them, somebody said they were waiting for darkness before the show could start with full lights.

To the left was a raised section of guest seats, filled with familiar people, a roped-off enclosure. Geoff pointed out a figure with glasses standing looking out at the hall. 'Dave Marsh', he said. 'Why don't you go and say hello?' So we went up and I shouted up to him, a good four feet above me: 'Mr Marsh!' He looked down and knelt down to listen. I stuck up my hand to him. 'Dan French – Point Blank'. 'Oh, yeah' he said, and shook hands. We chatted for a couple of minutes about the hall, and how we were here and got tickets, and then he said he had to go. 'Have a good show now.'

Geoff and I went back to our seats, near the back of the stalls. He got his camera and spare lens out of his rucksack. We agreed to sit where we were for the first half, and then go down the aisle near the front for the second set. When the lights went down, we both rushed as far forward as we could, as did a lot of other people! Before long the crowd was crushing together, and people were getting wedged against the loose, folding chairs, which were snapping like matches and being passed out over the sea of fans to the roadies at the side of the stage. Geoff and I were stuck in the middle, and the others nowhere to be seen. After what seemed like ages, there was the hum of the intro to 'Factory', and it was showtime again!

After both nights I hitched back to a small hotel with Geoff and Kristina; one night we got as far as the band's hotel (pretty central) with a couple of crew drivers, and then went on to our hotel which was further south (must book nearer the hall if I go again!). We sneaked out in the mornings since they'd only booked for two – decided we ought to leave separately and surreptitiously!

19 April 1981: Paris, Palais Des Sports St-Ouen

The worst thing about both nights was the crush, both before and during the show. The second night they wisely took the chairs out first (what were left of them from the previous scrum), but if anything it seemed fuller. I remember the familiar organ intro turning not into 'Factory' for once, but a strange new song about dreams (the live debut of 'Follow That Dream'). And both nights we were treated to the first performances of 'Can't Help Falling In Love', which I recognised from the Stylistics' version(!) – I fell in love with it at once, especially the breathtaking way it faded to the kick-start of 'Born To Run'. Whew! One of the funniest things was during 'Hungry Heart', when the crowd sang 'Everybody's got a hungry heart' for all four lines of the chorus, instead of 'You pay your money and you play your part' on the third line! And in 'Thunder Road', there was a faint response to Bruce's invitation to sing 'You ain't a beauty but hey you're alright' – the language barrier wasn't so obvious in Germany! 'You gotta practice,' joked Bruce the first time, and 'Close!' the second night!

I thought I'd take off with delight when the Medley ground to its usual halt only to be followed with 'Do you like good music?' Yeah! Yeah! I did – both nights! Still a favourite. And in the Medley on the second night we got treated to 'High School Confidential' – what a thrill! Despite a nasty scene outside when three American girls and some other fans were waiting to talk to Bruce when he came out after the show, only to be warned away with armed guards and guard dogs, those were my favourite two shows of the four I'd seen. I spoke to the 'little Gorilla' roadie when he came to see what the fuss was about outside, and said 'The French guys don't seem to understand – we always get allowed to wait for Bruce after a show.' He said, 'YOU don't seem to understand – this is a foreign country, and while we're here we have to follow the local rules.' The three girls were most upset, protesting 'We ALWAYS wait for Bruce!', close to tears. But we all had to leave – there was no point in trying to stay.

On Easter Sunday I hitched back to London, wishing I could have stayed and gone on to Barcelona, Lyon, Brussels, Rotterdam… But extremely happy that I had seen so many shows – three more than I expected to see – and all of Britain to come!! I wanted to go back with John H for Brussels, or the two Rotterdam shows, but they clashed with signing on(!) and I didn't want to risk being late a second time in a row. Mats E sent me a ticket for Gothenburg which I couldn't afford to use – would have cost £60 on the boat, return. I had to pay the rent, and had no savings. I still have the ticket – couldn't send it back in time. Next stop: Newcastle in May …

Gothenburg 1981 – 'the ticket that got away' – thanks anyway, Mats!

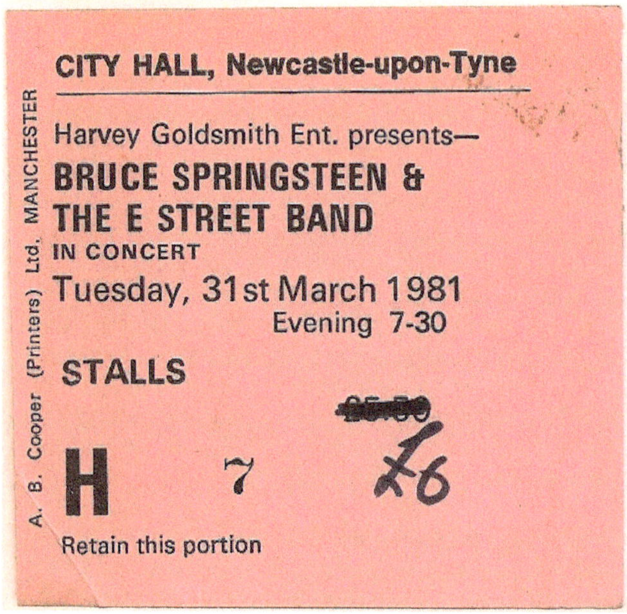

11 May 1981: Newcastle-upon-Tyne, City Hall

The UK leg of Bruce Springsteen's 1981 'River' tour was postponed from its original March-April period to May-June, leapfrogging over the continental European leg in April-May. The itinerary was expanded since the original announcement, increasing from four to sixteen shows in England and Scotland. Dates were re-ordered in the process, and the opening night shifted from Brighton to Newcastle. Here, like other dates first scheduled earlier, the tickets (and backstage passes) reflected the original timing, meaning that Newcastle tickets for 11 May 1981 all read 31 March 1981. Overall ticket prices increased in some cases in the interim, hence the handwritten '£6' replacing the crossed-out '£5.50' here. At the time, promoter Harvey Goldsmith's policy of introducing a 50p booking fee seemed to many an outrageous addition as a relative proportion of the basic ticket price. The hall was one of the smallest played in that era, at around 2,000 seats. Here Bruce first added an original new verse into 'This Land Is Your Land', in reference to the recent riots in Brixton, London.

13 May 1981: Manchester, Apollo Theatre

Rescheduled from its original date of 23 March, the first Manchester show was significant for the world premiere of 'Johnny Bye Bye', which my friend Rena overheard Bruce playing for Clarence in his dressing room. It was also soundchecked with the band, along with 'The Promised Land'. Also notable was the dedication of 'This Land Is Your Land' to the memory of Bob Marley, who had died that day in Florida. As in Newcastle, Bruce again featured his own line about 'the streets of Brixton' during the song.

The Manchester, Newcastle, Edinburgh and Brighton shows went on sale to personal callers at their respective box offices, as well as by the national postal application system Harvey Goldsmith offered. I went and queued overnight for Manchester tickets, reasoning that it was an easier journey from London than Edinburgh on the same on-sale date.

14 May 1981: Manchester, Apollo Theatre

The second show at Manchester was the shortest night of the whole European tour, as Bruce, by no means fully recovered from the exhaustion that caused the UK tour to be postponed, was struggling with a throat issue. By the end of a typical 3-hour concert at this time, he could often be seen being helped off stage by crew in the wings as the exhaustion kicked in.

As with the 1980 US leg and continental European dates, Bruce continued his tradition of picking a girl from the front of the audience to dance onstage during 'Sherry Darling' as part of the UK shows.

16 May 1981: Edinburgh, Playhouse Theatre

Bruce's first appearance in Scotland. Apart from the second show here the following night, Bruce only returned to this venue once in later years – during his solo acoustic 'Ghost Of Tom Joad' tour in 1996. The E Street Band would not play in Edinburgh again for 42 years, until 2023 at Murrayfield.

The personal ticket onsale at the Playhouse earlier in the winter was chaotic to say the least. Fans lined up overnight at the box office, but the management made the unexpected decision to open early for sales around midnight rather than at the advertised morning time. Unsurprisingly there was a sudden rush to get in, and some fans – including my friend Harry – who were wrapped in sleeping bags – got caught out in the stampede. Harry rolled in his sleeping bag down the steps beside the building. Luckily, he survived without injury, and was still able to buy tickets! When I heard his story, I was glad I'd opted to join the Manchester queue that night instead, which was relatively civilised. Having made some early connections in different cities through my fanzine, I was able to trade spare Manchester tickets for Edinburgh ones.

17 May 1981: Edinburgh, Playhouse Theatre

For the second show at Edinburgh, added after the first round of dates were rescheduled, the correct date – 17 May – was shown, along with a large '2' and 'Second show' on the tickets to distinguish these from the first night.

This show was the first one at which 'The Ties That Bind' was played as the opening song; 'Prove It All Night' was normally the most common opener otherwise at this time. Having previously had floor / stalls tickets, this time I experienced the view from the balcony, and so for the first time was able to fully appreciate the stage light show directed by Mark Brickman.

20 May 1981: Stafford, Bingley Hall

One of the later shows to be added, Stafford Bingley Hall was the first UK show to move from small theatres to medium sized venues, before the tour finished at larger indoor arenas. It may have been chosen as an alternative to a third concert at Birmingham. Coach trips were laid on from around the Midlands. The band's own tour itineraries also listed a second date here for 21 May, for which backstage passes – if not tickets – got as far as being produced, but the extra show was never publicly advertised or sold. Perhaps this was just as well, since the venue itself, despite being popular with other touring musicians, was effectively a concrete agricultural shed, and rock shows alternated with animal shows. I can remember seeing straw from a cattle event being swept out of the hall as fans were going in, and the aroma of cows lingered during the concert. I made likely the only circulating audience recording of this night, using my Dad's Dictaphone, and freely admit the result was only sufficient for historical interest!

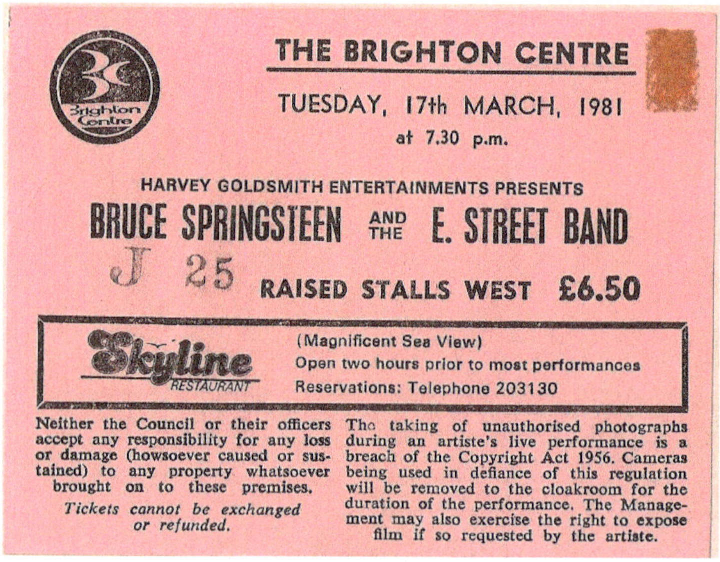

26 May 1981: Brighton, The Brighton Centre

Bruce only ever played two shows in Brighton. The first one was advertised locally and I missed the onsale, otherwise I would have gone in person, but luckily for me a friend helped me get a 'Raised Stalls West' ticket. This was initially planned as the start of the UK tour, meant as a warm-up show before London at the time. The cancellation and postponement of the UK leg happened so near the 17 March date that crew had arrived to begin setting up the stage when it happened. Other warm-up locations first considered but abandoned included St Austell and Southampton, according to radio DJ Roger Scott, no doubt influenced by rock itineraries such as for The Who. A rumour of a Who / E Street gig at The Venue in London was intriguing, but also never came to fruition. I was interviewed for *The Sunday Times* by Richard Williams, tipped off that I was one of a few fans aiming to go to all 16 UK shows.
At first sitting next to my friend and fellow fanzine editor Gary 'Candy's Room' Desmond, when I saw how easily people moved forwards in the dark once the show started, I excused myself and ended up much closer to the stage on the floor.

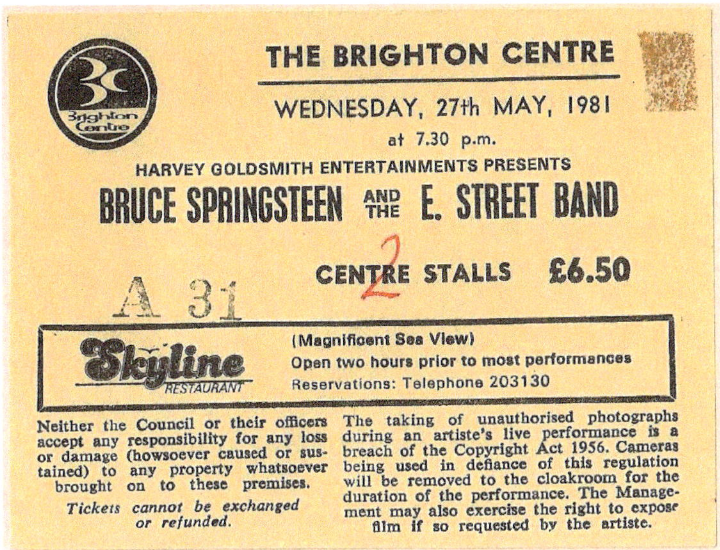

27 May 1981: Brighton, The Brighton Centre

The second Brighton show was announced in line with the rescheduled leg in May, and so tickets had the correct date. I heard about the personal onsale and again queued overnight, securing my best ever Bruce seats, near the centre of the front row. As with the second Edinburgh date, a '2' featured on these tickets. Whether it was the seaside location reminding Bruce of the Jersey Shore, or the last medium-sized (4,500 seats) venue before the move to arenas, or simply my spot, but this remains one of my all-time favourite shows, and I felt I'd earned my place after the onsale queue. I heard the security supervisor telling a few nervous-looking staff along the stage front: 'If they move – run!' So I knew we had a clear path to the stage itself as soon as the lights went down. Three hours later, I had bruises across my chest from being pressed up against the stage, but I was near enough to touch Bruce's boots when he was at the microphone, and when he opened up with 'Born To Run' I knew we were in for a special encore - the 1981 European debut of 'Jungleland'.

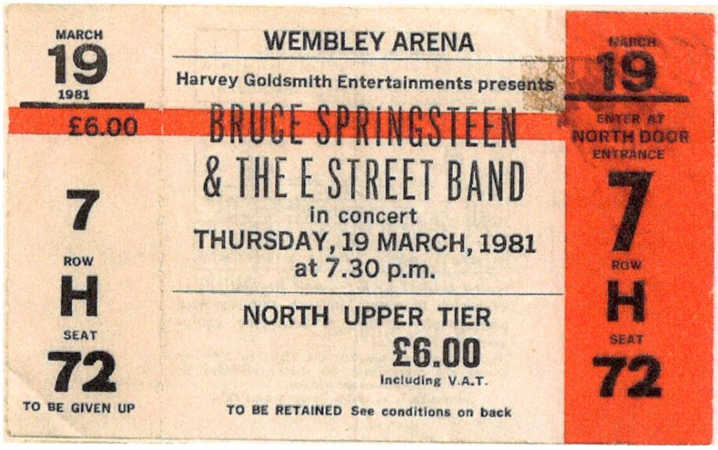

29 May 1981: London, Wembley Arena

The first night of six shows by Bruce and the E Street Band at the 8,000 seat Wembley Arena in London on the 'River' tour, the original dates having been rescheduled from March, and then added to. This stand was the first of the larger indoor arenas comprising the second half of the UK tour, finishing with two concerts at Birmingham NEC on 8 June, after a month on the continent and a month in the UK.

I was fully expecting to travel across town to the north London venue by public transport as I would do normally, but a different story awaited. Earlier in the day, I had an errand to run on behalf of my friend Rena with whom I'd shared the Frankfurt and Munich shows that April. She joined us for the early UK shows at Newcastle and Manchester (where she heard Bruce rehearsing 'Johnny Bye Bye' backstage for its live debut), but had to return to Germany before Wembley; and asked me to deliver a bouquet of flowers to Clarence as a welcome to London. So I went with my friend Mary to the Carlton Tower hotel in Knightsbridge, where Rena had told us the band were staying. We sat in the hotel foyer armed with the flowers, having asked at Reception for Mr Clemons - who else? - and I expected the lift doors to open and reveal The

Big Man, as he'd appeared in Frankfurt. We waited, but no sign of CC. Then we saw an elderly black couple emerge from the lift, looking around as if a bit lost and unsure what to expect. Mary and I looked at each other, both thinking: 'Mr Clemons Senior?' and Clarence's mother - it had to be! We went up to introduce ourselves, and sure enough, it was Clarence Snr and Thelma Clemons, the Big Parents (although not as big as CC).

Learning that The Big Man was already at the arena soundchecking early, we quickly decided to give the bouquet to his parents instead - 'Welcome to London!' They were utterly charming, and of course so proud of their son 'Clancy', as they called him. We were warmly invited to visit them at home in Norfolk, VA, 'any time'. With delightful genteel courtesy, they made sure we both had tickets for the show that night. 'Yes, thanks, we're all set.' 'And do you have a ride to the show?' Mary and I looked at each other again. 'Actually, now you mention it, we don't have any travel booked yet.' 'Well, you two meet us back here, and we'll give you a ride.' It felt like a unique opportunity - how kind, why not?

At the appointed time, Mary and I joined the Clemonses again, who took us to a minibus which sped us to Wembley Arena, along with Stevie's fiancée Maureen Santoro and various other band guests we didn't recognise. We were all driven in a side entrance and dropped off right inside the arena. 'Enjoy the show now!' said Clarence Snr and Thelma, as they waved goodbye. The next thing we knew, Bruce and the E Street Band were walking past us, and we realised that we were right behind the stage, and they were climbing stairs to get onstage. It was almost showtime! We had no passes to stay backstage, only our tickets, and couldn't watch the show from behind the stage anyway, so Mary and I had to find the nearest crew member and ask them to help us out from backstage - we needed to effectively get thrown out in order to get in to the main hall with our tickets for the show! We made it back inside again as 'Born To Run' was blasting from the stage, and the Wembley audience erupted in welcome to the band.

Having entered with the house lights down, we couldn't find our floor seats in the dark, so we found a space between seating blocks where we could stand, watch and wait for the intermission, and had a great time with room around us. Before the end of the first set, Bruce started something we didn't recognise, and it gradually dawned on us that here was the debut of an unknown song - 'Trapped'! We found out later that it was adapted from a Jimmy Cliff original, after Bruce found it on a cassette compilation at Amsterdam airport the previous month. Bruce's version ingeniously reworked the original reggae rhythm into a rock arrangement. Now we knew why Clarence and the band had needed extra soundcheck time. Finally, again, London was ready for Bruce Springsteen.

30 May 1981: London, Wembley Arena
(ticket stub thanks to Mike Saunders)

On 30 May 1981, having been delayed getting into Wembley Arena the previous night, I was determined not to be late a second time. Meeting my friend Neil at his home in Richmond earlier that day, we agreed to travel to Wembley together for the show. Impatiently, I kept encouraging Neil that we should leave so as to get there in good time, but he was very relaxed and kept saying there was no rush. Of course, we ended up running late, racing to get into the arena and realising that the show had started - we missed 'Prove It All Night' and got in part-way through 'The Ties That Bind'. As you can imagine, I made sure this didn't happen for the remaining four Wembley shows! 'Jackson Cage' was a European debut that night, and Bruce spontaneously added 'Twist And Shout' as the audience was already leaving. As elsewhere, Bruce came out after the shows and sat in a van to sign autographs for fans. In merchandise, there was a limited edition souvenir Wembley shirt, with the correct dates on the back, only sold in London (as well as the standard European t-shirt).

31 May 1981, London: with Mary and Neil – photo by John Marriott

From Asbury Park to Hyde Park... On 31 May 1981, during a day off after two of Bruce's six Wembley Arena shows on the UK leg of the 'River' tour, I celebrated my birthday with a few friends. Mary and John and I decided to go to Knightsbridge, as we knew from the E Street Band tour itinerary that was where the band were staying in London. At the Carlton Tower hotel, we bumped into Max Weinberg coming out of the coffee bar. Going in, we discovered the cheapest drink on the menu was fresh orange juice for £1.30. This was a fortune at the time, when you consider that concert ticket prices were only £6.00! So we just bought one between us, with three straws. Enjoying wandering around the area in fine weather, the three of us stopped at a local newsagent for some more affordable refreshments. We were in the shop when suddenly Mary dropped her snacks and ran out the door. Puzzled, John and I left our shopping too, and followed her. A little way up the road we could see her talking to a familiar-looking guy in a brown leather jacket, standing with his back to a lamp-post;

she was almost clinging to him, and waving frantically to us. It was Bruce! She told us afterwards she'd spotted him out of the shop window and 'recognised him by the backs of his boots' as he walked past - an extraordinary coincidence.

The three of us chatted with Bruce briefly, who seemed relaxed but looked tired after the two previous days; and just by chance, two other friends (Neil and Gary) then joined us, jaws dropping in disbelief at our companion. I remember Neil stuck his hand out and asked excitedly: "When are you going to play 'Be True'?" Bruce kindly posed for a few photos (thank goodness we had a couple of cameras between us), and then said he was going for a walk around Hyde Park before bed (this was early evening). Handshakes, smiles, waves and he was off. What could we all do but find the nearest pub to celebrate the most unexpected birthday gift? We laughed at the memory of the recent *Daily Mail* article which claimed that fans could never meet 'smart people's hero' Bruce, as he was supposedly constantly surrounded by aides. Lucky London town!

31 May 1981, London: Bruce with John, Mary and Neil

1 June 1981: London, Wembley Arena

The third of Bruce and the E Street Band's 6-night stand at Wembley Arena in London during the original 'River' tour. Rescheduled from the original date of 2 April, tickets and passes featured that date. This was one of my best seats, a front row one, as at the second Brighton concert.

2 June 1981: London, Wembley Arena

The 2 June show was rescheduled from 3 April, and again the tickets reflected this change. This fourth show at Wembley Arena was notable for a rare guest appearance during the spring shows, legendary guitarist Link Wray, who joined in for the European debut of 'I Fought The Law'.

Back of the souvenir t-shirt for the 1981 London stand at Wembley

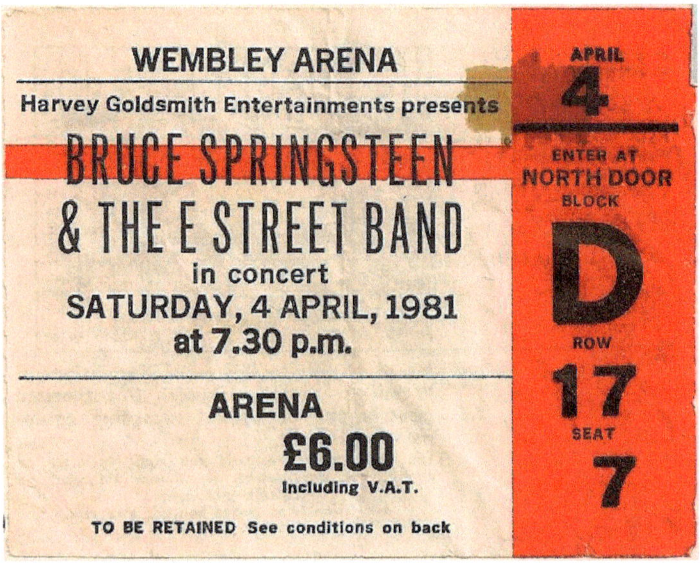

4 June 1981: London, Wembley Arena

The fifth Wembley concert was the last of the London stand to have the original date from April on its tickets and passes. The final three London shows had multi-track recordings, and there was a brief rumour of a live London EP being issued soon after, but nothing came of that. Thankfully, Nugs released the full concert as part of its Springsteen archive series, as it did for the last show on 5 June. Here the live recording immortalised three of the rare new songs from the 1981 season: 'Follow That Dream', 'Johnny Bye Bye', and 'Trapped'.

5 June 1981: London, Wembley Arena

Highlights of the London finale included the European debut of 'Here She Comes / I Wanna Marry You', the world debut of 'Jolé Blon', a reprise of 'I Fought The Law', and legendary US fan (also Springsteen housekeeper) Obie Dziedzic invited onstage for 'Sherry Darling'.

At this point I had been lucky enough to make it to 14 out of '16 The Hard Way', which I would complete two shows later at Birmingham. Even in the prime of youth at 23, the weeks of travelling, sleeping rough, hitch-hiking, eating at a subsistence level - literally living the life of a tramp - not to mention the physical experience of those amazing nights - caught up with me, and by this time I had 'tour fever': heavy cold, shaking limbs, constant exhaustion; but was determined to make it to the finish. I began to get a real appreciation of Bruce's own exhaustion issues, and I wasn't even performing! I wasn't alone; a few other fellow fans and friends had similarly followed the tour, and my friend John had done much the same as me AND worked a day job on top of it all.

After this triumphant end to the Wembley stand, John (who had a press pass for this night) and I met up again with our crew contact Glen Palmer, Clarence's assistant, to hang out briefly after the show. Glen took one look at us two, and told us that we looked terrible. We agreed - I'd spent some precious cash on an official tour souvenir scarf, as something to comfort the flu-like symptoms a little (I'd already bought one scarf earlier, which I sent to another friend), but it had little effect. Glen said: why don't you two take showers? You'll feel a lot better. We said, great idea, but how are we going to get a shower here, away from home, at Wembley Arena? Glen gave us towels and pointed us along a corridor. And so it was that John and I had showers backstage at Wembley - so welcome, and among the most refreshing showers I've ever had.

Standing in my shower stall, I noticed a couple of small items on the floor nearby, and out of curiosity picked them up. They were two guitar picks - clearly different types, and both worn from use. I assumed they probably fell out of the musicians' clothing as they stripped for showers there earlier. I have no absolute proof, of course, but it's not impossible that one was Bruce's pick, and the other Stevie's. That's my theory, anyway, and I'm sticking to it. (I no longer have the picks - I gave one to my girlfriend the following year, and the other to her sister, a big Stevie fan.)

Official Europe 1981 tour merchandise souvenir scarf

7 June 1981: Birmingham, National Exhibition Centre

On 7 June 1981, Bruce and the ESB played the 12,000 capacity NEC Arena in Birmingham for the first of their final two nights of the UK leg of the 'River' tour, and their largest venue in the UK at that time, having worked their way up from the 2,000 seat Newcastle City Hall a month earlier. Thanks to being able to sell a few copies of my 'Point Blank' fanzine during the tour, I made it to the 7th town and 15th show of the UK tour, with the end in sight (not that I was wishing for the end, despite exhaustion - but I was running on adrenaline by this point). This night featured two notable highlights: the European debut of 'Drive All Night', and a guest appearance by Pete Townshend, playing guitar on the final two encores. (Coincidentally, as with Link Wray's jam at Wembley on 2 June, no pictures have circulated of this live collaboration.) Once again, I was sitting near fellow tour veteran John, and when 'Drive All Night' started I looked over at him in the same row, expecting to see a look of bliss, as this was one of his favourite Bruce songs. Instead, I realised that John's month of combining tour-following with his day job had caught up with him - he sat leaning forward with his head resting on the railing in front of him, dozing through his only chance to hear the song that year. I remember being surprised at Pete Townshend's appearance as there was no announcement when he came on, and yet there was what looked very much like a second Miami Steve standing beside Stevie, complete with hat and braces. His unfamiliarity with the live performances showed at one point, I think during 'Detroit Medley', when Bruce stopped the band suddenly, and Pete, caught unawares, accidentally played an extra chord.

Note: Mike Saunders recollected the circumstances around Townshend's appearance:

'On May 26 and 27, as the rescheduled tour began its third week, Townshend finally made it down to Brighton to see Bruce. Nick Kent reported that Dave Marsh had arranged for him to attend, "along with a small coterie from The Who's office." The Springsteen fanzine Candy's Room later reported that Bruce, Marsh and Townshend spent time fishing at Roger Daltrey's trout farm in Sussex (presumably on their way to or from Brighton), and that Townshend attended the remaining eight shows of the tour at Wembley Arena (May 29/30, June 1/2, 4/5) and Birmingham NEC (June 7/8).
On June 7, after Bruce had dedicated The Promised Land to him earlier in the show, Townshend finally joined the E Street Band onstage, playing guitar on the final two encores, Born To Run and the Detroit Medley. Because he wasn't introduced, was clean-shaven at the time and wore a hat and braces that made him look like a Miami Steve clone, he wasn't easily recognisable and no pictures appear to exist of his guest appearance. Townshend recalled his Birmingham experience in Who I Am: "I played with Bruce as Stevie Van Zandt called out the chords. My role was to enforce the guitar part with Stevie by my side, while Bruce made that special connection with his audience. There is nothing quite like playing guitar with Bruce Springsteen on Born To Run, a hymn to breaking free."'

8 June 1981: Birmingham, National Exhibition Centre

Bruce and the band played their 16th and last show on the UK 'River' tour, the second of two nights at Birmingham. The tickets and passes showed 28 March, the original date before it was rescheduled. Backstage guests included Pete Townshend, who had played with the band the previous night after following the tour since Brighton. Townshend took Bruce for a celebratory night out in London the following day, including a U2 gig, before the conquering E Streeters headed home to continue rockin' all over America that summer.

Birmingham 8 June 1981: front row photo by Paul Markham

1982

The *'club-hopping'* tour

Bruce with Cats On A Smooth Surface, 1982 (unknown)

3 October 1982: Asbury Park, The Stone Pony (Cats On A Smooth Surface gig) (no ticket stub)

In September 1982, I visited Big Man's West in Red Bank, taken there with UK friend John by our Shore guide, Holly (RIP). There were some great photos of CC, Bruce, the E Streeters and others decorating the walls, and one bar was nicknamed 'Candy's Room'. Holly introduced me to the barmaid, who on learning I was a tourist from the UK, said: 'You wanna have what Bruce drinks?' She made me a Melon Ball cocktail (melon liqueur, vodka, and pineapple juice). I narrowly missed Bruce having a drink in the club that week, but was lucky enough to join Holly to catch Bruce jamming at The Stone Pony on his final appearance there that year, when he played for an hour with Cats On A Smooth Surface.

On 3 October, I was in Asbury Park, taking in the sights, seeing landmarks like Convention Hall and the Palace, in glorious weather. That night, Cats were due to play their regular weekend 3-set slot at The Stone Pony. Holly told us she was convinced Bruce, who had spent much of that summer playing a series of surprise 'club-hopping' appearances around the Jersey shore, had left for California to work on his next album. We decided to check out the Cats gig anyway, as it would give us the chance to soak up the atmosphere of the famous club where Bruce had so often played, and with that band too. Much to our surprise, after Cats had played their first set, word spread round the club that Bruce was at the bar - sure enough, there he was. I'd been chatting to a local regular ('Flash') earlier who asked if I wanted to meet Bruce, and of course I said yes, thinking: nothing to lose, but not expecting much - I hadn't wanted to bother him, as he was with his then girlfriend, a barmaid called Jenny. Flash soon came back to me and said 'The Boss will see you now' - so I followed him over, only to hear Flash tell Bruce: 'Hey Boss, this English guy wants to talk to you!' Squirming, I stuck out my hand and said Hi to Bruce, who luckily had had a few drinks, and was in a welcoming mood. He seemed highly amused that I'd come from England, and I got the chance to thank him for the 1981 shows I saw in Europe. I asked him if either Clarence or Stevie were planning to bring their bands to the UK anytime soon, and he said thoughtfully: not Clarence, but maybe Stevie (sure enough, I got home just in time to catch Little Steven's first Disciples of Soul show in London). He kept shaking my hand, and on the third time I took it as a sign to retreat, and left him in peace. Returning to Holly and John, we decided to position ourselves near the front, in case Bruce decided to join in for an encore or two. As Cats' second set was about to start, we heard an unmistakable voice onstage saying: 'Anybody got a guitar?' Before we knew it Bruce was strumming the opening chords to 'From Small Things...', laughing as the band scrambled to their instruments, and we were off for a full set of 14 songs, including the live debut of 'Open All Night', the rarity 'On The Prowl' and obscure covers like 'Rock Baby Rock It' (which Bruce taught the band in a few seconds). It was a marvel watching Bruce inspire this bar band, nodding to them to take solos, enjoying playing his favourite covers for fun, bursting with energy, looking like a lifeguard compared to the drawn, unhealthy figure we'd last seen in 1981. Just the best night and amazing luck, especially when we didn't expect the man to be around at all (indeed, it was his last major appearance that year before heading west), and of course the absolute highlight of our US trip. Not bad for just a few dollars, either.

1985

The *Born In The USA* tour

1 June 1985: Slane, Slane Castle

(IF I WERE YOU, I WOULDN'T START FROM HERE - text thanks to Mike Saunders)

The first point to make is that, despite endless listings of 'Slane Castle, Dublin' in the Springsteen reference books, Slane Castle is nowhere near Dublin. More like a medium-sized mansion with battlements, the castle actually stands beside the river Boyne in County Meath, some 35 miles northwest of the city in the heart of the Irish countryside. Faced with spiralling maintenance costs in the early 80s, owner Lord Henry Mountcharles had decided to bring in a bit of extra cash by allowing his grounds to be used for a series of massive annual rock concerts, most notably by the Rolling Stones in 1982 and Bob Dylan in 1984. Bruce's appearance, originally rumoured for the RDS, hung in the balance for some time before being officially confirmed in April 1985. Having borne the brunt of a disastrous riot after the Dylan concert, the residents of nearby Slane village had expressed strong objections to a further invasion by thousands of greasy-haired, denim-clad, drug-crazed, boozed-up, NME-reading, sheep-shagging, glue-sniffing rockers. They were eventually placated by assurances of tighter security and an apparent promise that Bruce's show would be the last to be held at Slane .... Until 1986, that is, when Queen played there, followed by Bowie in 1987 and more recently, Guns 'n' Roses. The villagers sold up and moved to Spaghetti Junction because it was quieter.

Bruce's Slane concert has an extensive series of 'firsts' associated with it. It was the first show of his 1985 European tour, his first show on this side of the Atlantic for almost 4 years, his first show in Ireland, his first outdoor show ever here, and the first European show by the new E Street Band with Patti and Nils. No doubt a total coincidence is the fact that it took place on June 1st and was show number 111 of the 'Born in the USA' world tour. Most importantly, however, it was Bruce's first giant, general-admission festival-style megagig. He'd played a handful of outdoor shows over the years (Red Rocks, Alpine Valley, Saratoga Springs, stadiums in Melbourne and Brisbane) but this was something else entirely, and the crowd at Slane were the guinea pigs. With numbers officially limited to around 65,000 (but widely reported to be closer to 100,000 on the day) this was by far the largest audience of Bruce's career at the time. It was to be a whole new experience both for him and us, which is why we had to be there.

Promoted by Jim Aiken in Belfast independently of Harvey '50p booking fee' Goldsmith in London, tickets for the Slane show were incredibly easy to come by, due to the size of the gig and the relaxed attitude at the Irish end. All this in direct contrast to the limited numbers available for Bruce's 1981 indoor tour. Having been used to overnight queues, unsuccessful postal applications and general frustration, many fans experienced intense guilt at having obtained a Slane ticket so easily, and had to endure extensive therapy once it was all over. The objects of desire were about 6 inches long, 2 inches wide...and blue, so it's not what you were thinking. Emblazoned along their length were the words 'Bruce Springsteen and the E Street Band' in silver lettering. The conditions included the usual 'No bottles, cans, tape recorders or cameras', but in recognition of the outdoor nature of the event, also stipulated 'No folding chairs or umbrellas'. Presumably hammocks, waterbeds, paddling pools and 3-piece suites were also prohibited, but they didn't say.

Exactly how our tightly-scheduled travel plans came together is long forgotten, but it took weeks of meticulous organisation, and at one point involved the hiring of a 40-seater coach until numbers dropped to a more manageable level. Joined by my friend Mick, I made my way up to London on May 30, staying overnight at Dan's place with his friend Neil. The four of us staggered out of bed in the wee small hours of May 31 (Dan's birthday) and caught a taxi to Euston by 5am. There we met

Tony (1) – who'd recently seen Bruce in Australia – and Robin. By 8.00am, we'd caught a train to Coventry and joined up with Tony (2) and Dave. A second train then took us via Birmingham (where we picked up Denise) to Liverpool Lime Street station, where we made our rendezvous at 10.30 with Jim, Jeff, Kev, Marge, Catharine and Janice – our token American. Enid Blyton's Famous Five had nothing on us. We were Bruce's Fabulous Fifteen Fanatics.

Amazed that we'd all come together exactly as planned, we divided ourselves up into a car and a 12-seater yellow minibus festooned with 'I'm a Rocker' stickers. This was to be our mobile home for the next 7 days and 1000 miles away we drove from Liverpool to Dublin to London to Newcastle and back to Liverpool. Dave and Jeff originally shared the driving, Dave subsequently taking over on a more-or-less permanent basis when Jeff revealed his potentially lethal habit of falling asleep at the wheel on dimly-it roads in the middle of the night.

We set off through the Mersey Tunnel and followed the coast of North Wales in blazing sunshine, passing picturesque villages, wide sandy bays, castles and rocky outcrops. Everything having gone like clockwork thus far, it was inevitable that Sod's law (anything that can go wrong, will go wrong) would come into effect before too long. Sure enough, as time grew short, we found ourselves stuck behind an agonisingly slow-moving tractor on the narrow road to Holyhead, eventually making it to the harbour just in time to catch the 2.45 Sealink ferry to Dublin.

The Irish Sea remained as calm as a millpond for the entire 3 ½ hour crossing. The ferry appeared to be gliding on air, heightening the dream-like quality of our journey, as the Welsh coast disappeared behind us and the rolling hills of Ireland loomed magically ahead in the mist. Below decks, the Irish experience began early when we encountered the confusing exchange rate between pounds and punts. Intending to pay in sterling for some packets of sandwiches, we were told that it was a better idea to change our money over first, and pay in punts. 'Although they will appear to cost more, it's actually less, and works out the same', said the girl at the counter, helpfully. It was a problem our travel-weary brains were unable to cope with. We took her word for it and retired to the bar. Several cans of Smithwick's later, we didn't care anymore. Years later, we're still not sure exactly what she meant.

We finally docked and drove onto Irish soil around 6.30, immediately finding the answers to the two most-asked questions by first-time visitors to the Emerald Isle – no, you don't need a passport, and yes, they do drive on the left. Feeling confident with 3 different maps of Dublin, we set off in search of our three pre-booked guest houses. Some while later, after several interesting circuits of the city centre and a variety of unplanned detours, short cuts, long cuts and straightforward wrong turnings, we found them. The majority of our group occupied two rooms in a cosy B'n'B which overlooked the North harbour, and the two large chimneys of the power station beyond. If you closed one eye and half looked away, you could imagine 'the gas fires of the refinery towers'. Then again, maybe not.

Suitably refreshed, we drove back into the city in search of food, passing on the way a half-demolished bakery wall with the remains of a sign offering the dubious delights of 'oven-fresh cak'. We declined the opportunity, preferring to sample traditional Irish cuisine at Flanagan's Pizza Parlour in O'Connell Street, just a few yards from the Gresham Hotel, where Bruce was staying. At the time, however, he was soundchecking at Slane, so no chance of a meet.

Also that evening, we carried out several sneak attacks on local newsagents, descending en masse upon our chosen target and stripping the shelves of anything featuring Bruce. In those bygone days of megastardom and total media overkill, he was everywhere, and it was a full-time team effort to check every music paper, national paper, local paper and magazine. Among our haul that evening was the Dublin Evening Herald, which had pictures of Bruce and Julianne arriving at the airport, and an interview with Jim Aiken about the setting up of the show. Undoubtedly the funniest front cover we encountered was that of the listings magazine 'What's on in Dublin' which used a spoof 'National Enquirer'-style design to advertise the career retrospective inside. 'Read about his hidden secret', it began, 'his favourite colour, his Nazi past, his groupie rating, the dawn fistfights with Kenny Rogers, and more!'

On the way back to our guest houses, the local radio station played the Nitty Gritty Dirt Band's version of 'Cadillac Ranch' and the closeness of the big day slowly began to dawn upon us. Following another mystery tour around the Dublin backstreets, we sank into our beds around half past midnight. It had been an exhausting 20-hour day, but the best was yet to come.

Four hours later, we were up again. Having abandoned plans to drive up to Slane the previous night in favour of a few brief hours of sleep, we agreed on an early start at 4.30am on what was now Saturday June 1 – Dave's birthday. Ignoring the carefully-laid breakfast table our landlady had prepared in advance, we piled into the minibus and set off in search of a 24-hour petrol station. By now, getting lost in Dublin was inevitable, all part of the fun and something we looked forward to. As we crossed the river Liffey for the umpteenth time, we switched on the radio in time to hear 'Trapped' (from the 'We are the World' album) blasting out.

While filling up, we decided to ask the taxi driver parked next to us for the directions to Slane. 'Well, the quickest way is to go up to those lights and turn right', he began. 'The only problem is you can't turn right there, 'cause you'll end up in the harbour'. Legend has it that he also said 'If I were you, I wouldn't start from here', but we can never be sure (makes a good title for this article, though). We thanked him for his help and, assuming he'd just got up to start a day shift, wished him 'top o' the morning' and said it looked like being a nice day. 'Is it fuck', he replied good-naturedly. 'I've been up all night, I'm off to me bed'.

We found the road to Slane without too much trouble, and headed North in the early morning light. As the outskirts of the city gave way to the fields, farms, trees and villages of the Irish countryside, it was hard to imagine that a vast rock concert could be taking place in such tranquil surroundings. The only indications that this was not an elaborate hoax on the part of Jim Aiken were the occasional yellow A4 signs fixed to trees which read 'Bruce Springsteen Concert'. Naturally, we took one.

As we travelled deeper into the idyllic landscape, the only vehicle on an otherwise deserted country road, we couldn't help but notice the large numbers of dead birds and small furry creatures scattered across the tarmac. Perhaps Ireland had a higher-than-average suicide rate amongst its indigenous wildlife. In which case, if the road was this quiet all day long, they must have to queue up in the bushes and jump, several at a time, under the wheels of the occasional tractor.

After around 20 miles, we encountered a police checkpoint. A small group of officers were sitting around chatting at the side of the road, one of whom came across to check that we had tickets for the show. We passed them out to him for inspection. "Sorry, lads" he said, poker-faced, "these are forgeries". We had a collective heart attack before, with natural comic timing, he continued "Only joking. Enjoy the show"! Breathing a giant sigh of relief, we drove on before he changed his mind. Bastard.

Two miles from Slane, we came across a second checkpoint. This was the end of the road as far as concert traffic was concerned, and only local residents could proceed further. Farmers were allowing the surrounding fields to be used as car parks for the day, charging £2 a vehicle. We pulled off the road and parked, our journey complete. It was still only 6 am. Grabbing our belongings, we set off on foot towards the village. The road wound gently down into the Boyne valley and crossed the river over an old stone bridge. As we stood there in the crisp dawn air, watching the water trickling gently along below us, the sun began to rise above the trees and break through the early morning mist. It was a haven of peace and tranquillity, a scene which probably hadn't changed much in the past few hundred years. Very much a fairytale setting, but cold hard reality was waiting for us on the other side.

We walked slowly up the other side of the valley into the outskirts of the village. It was then we discovered that we were not quite the first to arrive. A number of fans, traders and experienced boozers had turned up the night before, and the local pubs had apparently been open all night helping them to overcome their unquenchable thirsts. The results of this all-night session were all around us – lifeless bodies huddled in sleeping bags at the side of the road or laid out on garden walls. Those still able to stand staggered zombie-like towards us, searching for a suitable ditch to collapse into. Further down the road, others had camped out in the fields, reportedly tearing the doors from the portable toilet blocks provided to use as firewood during the chilly night.

'Bossopoly' game banknote, designed by Dave Percival

We continued on our way, following the stone perimeter wall of the castle grounds. This eventually gave way to a long section of temporary corrugated iron fencing which led us to the main entrance of the concert site, across which a large tarpaulin sheet had been stretched (this was not a state-of-the-art operation). A row of security barriers and some mean-looking guard dogs put paid to any thoughts of taking a quick look inside. We joined a small group of others at the front of the queue and sat down. It was now 7 am, a mere 8 hours before the 'gate' was due to open. As the morning ticked slowly by, the sun rose in a cloudless sky and the crowd grew larger, queuing peacefully 3 or 4 deep either side of the entrance and down the road in both directions for as far as the eye could see, and then some. Some members of our group passed the time by playing Bossopoly, a specially-adapted form of Monopoly featuring place names like E Street, Thunder Road, Mansion on the Hill, My Father's House and 10th Avenue, and using alternative banknotes with Bruce's face on them to complete the effect.

Now and again, small groups of us walked off to investigate the army of unofficial merchandise stalls which had opened for business at the roadside, selling all manner of stickers, badges, posters, t-shirts (we counted up to 40 different designs) and programmes. While chatting to one programme seller, we jokingly questioned the authenticity of his obviously home-made produce. "That's not official", we said. "Isn't it"? he replied, appearing genuinely surprised. We bought one anyway, just for posterity, because printed on the front cover were the immortal words 'Bruce Springsteen, Slane Castle 1th June 1985'. Maybe the guy had his own special language (firth, second, thirst, ford, fist, etc), or perhaps he just had a lisp, but his error stuck in our minds. Because of this, we will always remember Slane as the Firth o' June.

Back in the queue, a steward was summoned to sort out the problem of gatecrashers. "Right, all those who just pushed in, go to the back", he shouted hopefully. Naturally, nobody moved. "No problem", he smiled, and moved on. Around 12 o'clock, some frenzied activity at the front signalled that the tarpaulin sheet was about to be opened 3 hours early. Security staff began the thankless task of tearing each ticket down the perforation and throwing the stubs in a large bin. Except mine, that is. The guy who took my ticket ripped it clean in half through the silver lettering and threw both halves in the bin, leaving me with nothing.

Once we were inside, a breathtaking panorama opened up

before us. From the entrance, the vast cow pasture which formed the concert venue sloped steeply, then more gently down to the river Boyne, flowing peacefully across the site in the middle distance. At the bottom of the hill, backing onto the river, stood the giant stage, flanked on either side by massive PA stacks and video screens. Trees bordered the area and covered the slopes of the opposite bank. To the right, dominating the scene, stood the castle. It was a truly beautiful setting, and the weather was perfect. Pausing momentarily to take it all in, we ran down the hill as U2's 'Pride' played over the PA.

Panorama of arrival at Slane Castle – photos thanks to Jim Page

Fearing a crush at the very front, we based ourselves directly in front of the mixing tower, itself a multi-storey building which could have housed several families. Accommodating the sound desk, spotlights and a video cameraman, it was connected to the stage by a long umbilical cord of wires, slung high above the crowd. The stage itself was multi-levelled and had no backdrop, enabling us to see across the river. Catwalks extended out at either side for Bruce to run along, and extra sets of back-up speakers had been positioned at intervals further up the hill. Various official merchandise stalls, food and drink vendors, toilet blocks and first-aid posts hugged the perimeter. We settled down to begin the 5-hour wait until showtime, with the boiling sun now directly overhead and a cool breeze blowing down the valley.

As the afternoon wore on, the music on the pre-show tape was occasionally drowned out by the roar of helicopters ferrying band members and VIP guests into the backstage area. Soon, the site was a colourful mass of humanity, packed with fans from the stage right back up the hill to the road, with barely a blade of grass visible. It was an amazing sight, at once both exciting and overwhelming. We pinched ourselves to see if we were dreaming.

At 4 o'clock, Jim Aiken announced that Bruce would be onstage at 5. This proved to be the signal for the dream to turn into a nightmare. The natural slope of the site, combined with the inevitable human desire to move closer, soon resulted in a dangerous crush at the front. When Bruce hit the stage at 5 o'clock, thousands more surged forward, increasing the pressure and causing a steady stream of limp bodies to be pulled over the barrier. A large number of those pushing forward appeared to be mindless drunks; eyes rolling as they staggered into the crowd. The front began to turn ugly, with idiots forcing their way towards the stage, and battle-scarred victims fighting their way out of the chaos. The previous week's Heysel stadium tragedy was still fresh in the mind, and although there were no serious injuries at Slane, the potential for disaster was always obvious, prompting questions about the safety of such huge shows.

Our decision to stand in front of the mixing tower proved to be a lifesaver, as we were spared the pressure from behind and could maintain our position without being carried forward into the mob. The continual crowd movement, however, ensured we had to stay constantly alert in order to avoid being pushed, shoved, trampled and generally abused. Faced with the distractions of this endurance test, the actual concert became a secondary consideration. It was almost as if Bruce was playing the background music to the second battle of the Boyne.

The conditions in front of the stage were not lost on those behind the scenes, either. At one point, Jon Landau appeared at one side looking concerned, while Bruce himself asked the crowd to move back on a couple of occasions, his requests falling on deaf ears. There was actually very little the security staff could do to reduce the crush, beyond training hosepipes on the crowd to combat the effects of the searing heat. At one point, there were so many water droplets in the air that a mini-rainbow formed above our heads, one of the day's more striking images.

The show itself passed by in a blur. As we struggled to maintain balance and sanity, Bruce performed a comparatively short 26 song set which lasted for 2 hours and 50 minutes, with a 30-minute interval. Appearing punctually at 5, he was off for the last time at 8.20. The song selection was fairly typical of the latter stages of the 'Born in the USA' tour, consisting mostly of material from 'Born in the USA', 'The River' and 'Darkness on the Edge of Town', plus regular non-album inclusions like 'Trapped', 'Pink Cadillac' and the closing medley of 'Twist and Shout/Do you Love Me'? Essentially no surprises, except that is for Bruce's choice of first encore. Making brief reference to having had an Irish grandmother, he treated us to a solo electric version of the Beach Boys' 'When I Grow Up To Be A Man' – a performance which remains exclusive to Slane.

Throughout the show, Bruce sweated a lot, ran out along the catwalks several times, sang with Patti, kissed Clarence, danced with a girl from the audience, turned his baseball cap back to front and walked to the back of the stage to wave at the fans perched in the trees on the other side of the river, watching the show for free. They definitely had the right idea. Although their position was somewhat precarious, they were probably a lot more comfortable than we were.

The use of video screens for the first time at Slane was a mixed blessing. They were undoubtedly a great help in enabling those at the top of the hill to see what the ants on stage were actually doing, but from that distance, the pictures would have been 3½ days out of sync with the sound. Ironically, they proved to be the greatest help to us near the front. Unable to see very much of the events onstage, thanks to the constant movement and the inevitable presence of tall bastards directly in front of us, we ended up watching most of the proceedings on the screens. Having been used to seeing the E Street Band dressed in dark suits on the 'River' tour, it was a stark contrast to see them wearing brightly coloured shirts for maximum noticeability. The sight of Roy Bittan actually dancing lingers in the mind, as does Nils Lofgren's huge Styrofoam Stetson (worn during 'Cadillac Ranch'), and the use of a panoramic view of the Boyne flowing into the distance during – what else – 'The River'. This image was subsequently used to illustrate the song for the remainder of the tour.

As the final strains of 'Twist and Shout' died away, the massive crowd began to disperse and we regrouped to count our bruises, realising we'd survived the event unscathed. Deciding to rest and relax until the majority of the fans had gone, we were able to witness the aftermath of the frontstage chaos. The ground was a sea of rubbish – paper, discarded clothes and thousands of empty plastic bottles. As the roadies set about dismantling the stage, drunks crawled through the wreckage on their hands and knees, shaking the bottles in the hopeless search for more alcohol. Further up the hill, oblivious of the world around them, a couple were attempting some kind of drunken sexual congress while remaining fully clothed.

One of the strangest remnants we found in the mud was a broken telephone dial. This prompted several theories. Perhaps at one point there had been a public phone box near the stage which had been demolished in the rush. What if there had been someone inside? We imagined his last moments on the phone: 'Hello darling, it's me. I'm in Slane. Had a good journey over. Weather's wonderful and everything's really peaceful. The guy's just said Bruce will be on in an hour, and...AAAAAGH!'

Around 9.30, as the sun set behind the castle and the evening chill set in we began to make our way back, dragging our sunburnt skin and aching bones up the hill with considerably less energy and enthusiasm than we'd had when running down some 9 hours earlier. The road was a solid mass of bobbing heads disappearing into the distance like the start of the London marathon. Progress was slow as we made our way back across the old stone bridge and up towards the car parks, which all looked the same in the dark. When we first arrived, the area had been virtually deserted. Now, the fields were packed with cars, the road was lined with around 50 coaches, and 100,000 people were attempting to leave Slane all at once on the same narrow country road. Needless to say, traffic was at a standstill and looked like staying that way for the next few years.

We finally found the yellow minibus around 11pm, deciding to let the worst of the jam clear itself before we made a move, having first cleared away the broken glass which some thoughtful individual had placed in front of our tyres. Just as we'd begun to consider crashing out in the bus until morning, a gap appeared in the gridlock and we made it back to the guest house by around 2am after a shattering 22-hour day. Heads hit pillows and sleep came almost immediately.

The next morning, we allowed ourselves the luxury of a lie-in until at least 8 or 9 o'clock before going down to breakfast. Somewhere along the way, we'd picked up an extra person. Rather than eyeing them suspiciously and demanding instant payment, our landlady simply said 'Jeez, I coulda sworn there was one less of you yesterday. Never mind, I'll lay another place.' As we crunched cornflakes and discussed the Slane experience, she casually enquired 'Did you enjoy the match, boys?' We nodded, too tired to explain.

It was now June 2 and, regrettably, time to make our way back to England. Due to various complications, we were set to return via the southerly route from Rosslare to Fishguard, and had most of the day to kill before catching the late ferry across. Around 12 o'clock, having raided a couple more newsagents for Slane reviews in the Sunday papers, we made our last few circuits of Dublin city centre and headed south down the east coast of Ireland in blazing sunshine. En route, we stopped at Wicklow, taking time out to explore the bars, the shops and the beaches.

Fuelled by alcohol, our brains frazzled by the sun and our bodies in the terminal stages of Slane-lag, it seemed that every bend in the road brought fresh absurdity and hilarity.

Passing through one particularly crowded spot, we witnessed a group of people attempting to push a broken-down car up a hill backwards. 'Take the handbrake off!' shouted one. 'Don't be stupid, it'll roll downhill!' replied the driver. Stopping to fill up at a garage further down the road, we noticed that the office window displayed a VISA sticker, under which had been placed a contradictory handwritten sign which read 'No credit'. Obviously, all major credit cards were accepted, as long as you paid by cash.

The inhabitants of Courtown revealed a fondness for surreal signs and instructions. Pinned to the narrow doorway of a shop in the high street was a notice which stated 'No go-karts allowed'. Quite how a go-kart would be able to squeeze through without losing all four wheels was beyond us. Exactly why a go-kart driver would want to destroy his vehicle by attempting to enter the shop was another matter entirely. Down towards the beach, we encountered a further confusing message which warned 'Don't throw your ice-cream in the river'. This could have meant that the local council was on an anti-pollution drive, but worked equally well as a simple public service announcement: 'If you throw your ice-cream in the river, you may find it soggy and difficult to eat afterwards.'

First prize for weirdness, however, went to the push-button hand drier which only operated if you kept the button depressed. This meant that rubbing both hands together under the warm air jet was impossible. Keeping the button down with one hand, users had to wait for the air to blow the drips slowly off the other hand before swapping over. (We half-expected to find someone sitting on a tree branch, sawing it away from under themselves, but no luck there.)

Arriving in Rosslare, we reluctantly boarded the ferry and went up on deck to watch the coast of Ireland disappearing slowly into the sunset. Although we'd only been in the country for two days, we'd definitely got the bug, and had fallen in love with the people, their unfussed approach to life, their hospitality, generosity, unique sense of humour and illogical logic. The Guinness wasn't bad, either. Vowing to return one day, we sailed off into the night, on our way to Bruce's two shows in Newcastle, but that's another story

Slane made headline news just about everywhere. Quite apart from extensive coverage in a variety of Irish papers and the fortnightly music magazine Hot Press, there were also reports in the Mirror, Sun, Star, Mail and Express, reviews in the Times and the Guardian and features in Melody Maker and Rolling Stone, among others. The final word on Slane, however, belongs to Clarence Clemons. Remembering the world tour for a Rolling Stone article in 1986, he described the helicopter trip up to the site, and spoke of his awe at the sight of the 100,000 fans spread out on the hill below. 'It wasn't only the sheer volume of numbers,' he continued, 'but the sheer volume of harmony and peace.' I wish I could have a pint of whatever he'd been drinking, because from where we were standing, the only harmony in existence was Patti Scialfa's hairspray.

And so ends this version of the Slane legend. Some of us made it over for Bruce's 1988 show, and others in 1993 and later, but Slane will remain a unique experience for all involved. Never mind all that though, where did I put my Guinness...

Most of the 'Slane Survivors', Irish coast – thanks to Jim Page

4 June 1985: Newcastle-upon-Tyne, St James' Park

Having left Ireland on 2 June, our travelling group of 'Slane Survivors' made it via a few hours' sleep at my place in London to Newcastle on 3 June, thanks to our drivers Jim, Dave and Jeff. After delivering most of us to a B&B in town, Dave had to drive again to get me to my base, my girlfriend's house near the coast! Quite the epic road trip for us since 31 May. This was the first of six shows in the UK in 1985, all outdoors.

Bruce continued his regular tradition of charitable social support at tour stops, in this case donating a cheque for $20,000 to the Northumberland and Durham Miners' Support Groups, having met some wives of unemployed local miners coping with a year-long industrial dispute.

5 June 1985: Newcastle-upon-Tyne, St James' Park

Mike Saunders wrote: *'We did get … the rarely-played Vietnam-themed B-side "Shut Out The Light", which Bruce prefaced with his story about how he met "Born On The Fourth Of July" author Ron Kovik. This was particularly special as it was dedicated to Paul Lucas, one of the travelling family of Springsteen fans I'd recently met and was standing close to at that moment. He'd met Bruce at the soundcheck on 3 June and given him a copy of the book "Dispatches" by Vietnam war correspondent Michael Herr. Paul's request for "Shut Out The Light" was met with "maybe second night", and so it was. On the bootleg tape that later circulated, multiple strangers who didn't have a clue who he was can be heard cheering anyway with us. This was later noted in a review by pop magazine "No. 1": "Bruce dedicates a song 'to Paul, if you're out there'. 10,000 people cheer and wave. Are they ALL called Paul?"'*

15 June 1985: Frankfurt, Waldstadion

My original plan for 1985 included taking all of June off to follow the continental European tour, but this was thwarted when I got called up for jury service in London, potentially clashing with most of the month. After a week or so in court, I became physically sick out of extreme frustration, and had to plead to be excused from continuing the service. I recovered enough just in time to make a flying dash to Frankfurt and back on a mid-month weekend, still feverish but determined to salvage something from my summer plans. By the time I got into the Waldstadion, it was almost full to capacity, so I ended up having a view of the whole stadium from the very back, including the experience of a weird brief delay between the action and the sound, due to audio relay towers. No wonder my memory of that show is something of a fever dream.

29 June 1985: Paris, Parc De La Courneuve

Tickets and posters for the two Paris shows all showed the original venue, Stade De Colombes, but after a football riot in Brussels, authorities moved both events to the large field of Parc De La Courneuve in the northern part of the city.

Attending both shows with Dave & Francoise was memorable if challenging for us all – Francoise needed a wheelchair, and little provision was made then for anyone with impairments, so we just had to make the best of it. As the park was quite a way out of town and transport back to the centre was limited, Dave and I ended up taking turns to carry Francoise at times.

30 June 1985: Paris, Parc De La Courneuve

The 1985 tour being Bruce's third foray to Europe after 1975 and 1981, by now he was becoming confident enough in foreign parts to attempt a few words and phrases in local languages, and so in Paris he used 'Bonjour', 'Merci', and even 'Comment ca va?' References to Paris and France also featured in Bruce's song introductions and spoken sections.

The second show on 30 June took place under a near full moon, and during 'Ramrod' this inspired Bruce to channel his inner werewolf: 'Almost got a full moon tonight (howls)...' Since then, we noted that it seemed 'full moon shows' often seemed to bring out something extra in Bruce's performances.

3 July 1985: London, Wembley Stadium

1985 saw Bruce's first outdoor shows in the UK, a trend which would continue on many tours here since. Fans listening from outside to the soundcheck heard an unfamiliar new song which turned out to be 'Seeds', premiered that night and repeated at the following two London concerts. A welcome surprise guest at all four of the UK shows was Little Steven, who joined in for the final encores each time.

As well as the outdoor experience, this was UK fans' first experience of general admission – no reserved seats or pit for years to come. In the crush, a big fight broke out near the front. One night, an audience member somehow climbed on top of the fragile canvas stage roof.

4 July 1985: London, Wembley Stadium

Three shows at Wembley Stadium meant a lot of media coverage, especially for the 'Independence Day'-themed 4th of July date. An accordion was visible on stage, which prompted speculation that maybe we would be treated to '4th Of July, Asbury Park (Sandy)', but instead Bruce marked the occasion with a unique acoustic performance of 'Independence Day'. 'The Promised Land' was dedicated to U2 ('Bono and the guys'), who Bruce had first met in London at the end of his last visit in 1981.

CBS produced miniature promotional 'Springsteen passports' to commemorate the London shows.

6 July 1985: London, Wembley Stadium

Bruce played two European debuts at the third Wembley 1985 show: 'Highway Patrolman', and ('especially for London') a cover of local boys The Rolling Stones' 'Street Fighting Man' in the encores, which featured Little Steven guesting again. Gate opening time on 6 July - a Saturday - was two hours earlier than previously 2pm, with the show due to start at 4pm, but actually running at least half an hour late.

It's long been believed that Bruce's Wembley stage was left behind to be used at Live Aid a week later, since he used a different stage for the next concert at Leeds, but this has never been publicly confirmed by Harvey Goldsmith who promoted both events.

7 July 1985: Leeds, Roundhay Park

Being the day after the third Wembley show, this meant swift travel was needed to get from London to Leeds in time, and our group following all the UK shows just made it (a similar experience took place in 2013, when Leeds was the date after Cardiff). Another weekend date, the gates opened at 1pm and the show was set for 4pm.

The venue being a field echoing Slane the previous month, security was vulnerable and quite a few fans broke through the perimeter fence and added to the crush near the front, delaying the second half of the show after its interval.

Highlights included 'Racing In The Street' (also performed at the first Newcastle concert), the sole European appearance of 'Follow That Dream', and a farewell cover of John Fogerty's 'Rockin' All Over The World', first heard regularly during the 1981 European tour and occasionally on later tours, almost always only outside the US. Little Steven made his fourth UK guest appearance that week for the final encores again.

1988

The *Tunnel Of Love Express* tour

1 April 1988: Uniondale, Nassau Coliseum

My first time seeing Bruce and the E Street Band on tour in an arena in the US (my first Bruce gig in the US had been at The Stone Pony in 1982). Jeremy arranged a commission to review the concert for a UK music paper, which meant two complimentary press tickets for the first Nassau date on 1 April. I remember the journey out to Long Island and being surprised that the Coliseum seemed in the middle of nowhere, surrounded by a vast car park.

It was our introduction to the unusual 'Tunnel Of Love Express Tour' format, for which Bruce moved band members around on stage, and presented a fairly static set list – with the welcome inclusion of a fair amount of material not experienced in Europe on previous tours, both from the 'Tunnel Of Love' album and other rarities and covers. The addition of the 'Horns Of Love' brass section gave the show something of a soul / R'n'B revue feel, echoing 1976-1977.

Unusually, we had a view from behind the stage – actually a welcome different perspective, getting a 'band's eye view' of events. One remarkable moment was when an over-enthusiastic fan jumped on stage during 'She's The One'; Bruce grabbed him by the shirt and flung him bodily into the arms of security staff in the wings. Even without seeing his facial expression, we tensed at the change in atmosphere, not having witnessed what seemed like anger from Bruce. Luckily nobody else tried their luck doing that for the rest of the night.

2 April 1988: Uniondale, Nassau Coliseum

Having collected our press tickets for the first show from Jon Landau's office in Manhattan, we reckoned we had nothing to lose by asking if tickets for the second night were available, and were delighted at the chance to buy these easily on the spot, and have an extra concert during our trip. A very similar set, but a different view, and no stage invasion this time. I was grateful to hear new tracks such as 'Walk Like A Man' at these shows, which didn't get played later in Europe.

Nassau Coliseum, April 1988, photo by Jeremy Benson

23 May 1988: New York City, Madison Square Garden

The final night of the stand in New York City on the Tunnel of Love tour, 1988, and my first time at Madison Square Garden. Approaching my 30th birthday, I'd flown to the US for the last two shows without any tickets, and got shut out the previous night, but made it to the finale. Eternal thanks to my dear friend Holly (RIP) for the ticket! Knowing I'd missed out on the 22nd, she was determined to make my trip worthwhile, and came up to me minutes before showtime – in the drop-line of hopefuls outside the arena – pushed a ticket into my hand, and just said: 'Run!' I rushed in and found my seat just as the lights went down.

It was a noticeably looser show than at Nassau Coliseum in early April, with fresh additions like 'Boom Boom' and 'Have Love Will Travel'. I remember drummer Max (accidentally?) starting a different song before Bruce switched to 'Vigilante Man'. Barbara Carr and Jon Landau guested on stage, during 'You Can Look (But You Better Not Touch)' and the encores respectively. A rare cover of 'Lonely Teardrops', which I missed the previous night, was an unexpected final delight – later I caught its only other performance, at Sheffield that July.

19 June 1988: Paris, Hippodrome de Vincennes

Once again in Paris for Bruce with Dave and Francoise, we enjoyed a meal the previous night near the Chateau de Vincennes, quite unaware that Bruce and Clarence were guesting on stage at the 'SOS Racisme' benefit nearby.

The Hippodrome is a flat horse-racing track, 60,000 capacity. As in 1985, with Francoise in a wheelchair, we chose the only practical spot for a (distant) view, on a raised rim of ground around the track. Coincidentally, I randomly bumped into two people I met at the New York shows that May.

21 June 1988: Birmingham, Villa Park

Bruce's first 1988 UK shows gained much media interest, including Midlands TV: presenter Gary Hudson filmed a faked breakfast of local fan-friends including Springsteen book author Chris, 'The Fever' fanzine Dave and fiancée Francoise, who met through a mutual love of Bruce, all hosted by Chris's mother Winni, the star of the news clip shown that day.

Midlands TV news video shoot with local fans Chris Hunt, Dave & Francoise, 'Max' Soden, 'Miami' Ronnie Cowell and Clive Mottram

Adding to the VIP effect, when there was a problem for Francoise crossing train platforms en route to the concert, a very helpful station manager arranged for a goods train carriage to be shunted between platforms, so she could cross over in her wheelchair with us – unthinkable measures these days!

This stage of the tour was transitional, as with the shift to outdoor venues, Bruce began to drop some of the more intimate songs that he'd played in indoor arenas earlier, in favour of crowd-pleasers, but not before the final tour performances of 'One Step Up' and Woody Guthrie's 'Vigilante Man' – I'd caught two of the four times the latter was played.

Francoise & Dave's private goods train carriage; local show poster

22 June 1988: Birmingham, Villa Park

At the second of the two Villa Park shows, Edwin Starr - who had moved from the US to live nearby in the Midlands – guested on 'War'. Covers of 'Who Do You love' and 'Have Love Will Travel' made their UK live debuts here, as alternatives from the previous night. A local girl invited from the audience to dance onstage promptly took her top off, causing Bruce to react: 'I thought you English were supposed to be kinda reserved!'

25 June 1988: London, Wembley Stadium

Bruce played a rare cover of 'Love Me Tender' towards the end, an affectionate nod to the now familiar capital city. In his introduction to 'Born To Run', he reminisced about the band's first nervous visit to England, playing Hammersmith Odeon in London, and musing on the search for home and community.

The soundcheck was unusual: 'Twenty-Five Miles' was rehearsed with Edwin Starr, who repeated his guest appearance from the previous show in Birmingham – but on 'War' again, instead of the soundchecked cover. Also tantalisingly tested were Nanci Griffiths' 'Gulf Coast Highway' and 'Across The Borderline' (Cooder / Hiatt / Dickinson) which reportedly Bruce had become obsessed with on the tour, and Jackie Wilson's 'Lonely Teardrops'. Only the last song would eventually appear in the UK later that summer.

7 July 1988: Dublin, RDS Jumping Enclosure

Bruce's first show in Ireland since the notorious Slane Castle event in 1985, and thankfully a more civilised contrast with that craziness, at a smaller outside venue, part of the RDS multi-purpose sports complex in Dublin itself. The success of this choice meant an ongoing relationship with the same venue for many successive tour visits over the years.

Bob Dylan's 'Chimes Of Freedom' was a recent and now regular addition to the setlist, following Bruce's announcement of his participation in the forthcoming 'Human Rights Now!' concert series for Amnesty International. He introduced the song making reference to Amnesty's work and its idea of freedom. 'Paradise By The C' frequently featured this season.

9 July 1988: Sheffield, Bramall Lane

As Brucebase recounts: '"Spare Parts" from this show was officially released on 12" and CD EP later that year - without the introductory story. However, "Spare Parts" on the *Video Anthology* VHS/DVD does include the story, overlaid with shots from around Bramall Lane.' This marks the first time footage from a UK concert was featured in a Springsteen video.

Although I met many lovely people at the show (hi Linda), I couldn't locate one key person I was trying to find, who'd arranged a lift and accommodation. Along with other temporarily 'homeless' friends Tony and Lisa, I followed Mike to his B&B, The Peace Guest House, to take shelter for the night. Despite it being high summer, we were wet from rain and cold by the time we tried to get some sleep, ransacking the single room for any spare fabric we could fashion into bedding, such as the tablecloth. Three of us huddled shivering on the floor meant we rattled the wardrobe door, adding to the sleeplessness. We sneaked out next morning while Mike went to breakfast, where he encountered a fight taking place – so much for the 'peace' promised! Lisa and I enjoyed a hot reviving breakfast at Sheffield station – British Rail bacon sandwiches never tasted so good.

'Sleeping rough' on the floor of The Peace Guest House - photo and emergency shelter thanks to Mike Saunders

Ad for the two Sheffield shows, July 1988

10 July 1988: Sheffield, Bramall Lane

Having booked proper accommodation at The Rutland Arms pub nearer the station, the second night at Sheffield was much more comfortable. Highlights of the show included rarities 'Roulette', 'Can't Help Falling In Love' and Jackie Wilson's 'Lonely Teardrops', their only UK appearances in 1988. A 34-song set including 11 encores made for a fitting farewell to the UK for the summer tour, and we could look forward to a return to London in the autumn as part of the upcoming 'Human Rights Now!' tour.

The Rutland Arms pub, Sheffield 10 July 1988

12 July 1988: Frankfurt, Waldstadion

After Sheffield, I continued the tour with four shows in Germany and Switzerland, thanks to a road trip with Margrit ('Maggie') from Hamburg, and Lisa visiting from Florida. While the Frankfurt concert was a return to the outdoor Waldstadion where I'd been in 1985, I took the chance to get a snap at the Festhalle arena, site of my first Bruce show in 1981.

Frankfurt July 1988 – photos thanks to Margrit or Lisa

14 July 1988: Basle, Fussballstadion St Jakob

My first time visiting Switzerland, and as so often with its geographical location, the audience was mainly a combination of Swiss, Italian, French and German fans. 'Follow That Dream' was a request.

Road trip: Vera from Munich (RIP), Lisa and Margrit

17 July 1988: Munich, Olympia-Reitstadion Riem

All aboard for Munich: Lisa, Wolfgang, Thomas, and Margrit

Unlike in 1981 when I only spent a few hours in Munich around the show, a hasty same-day visit, in 1988 we had time to experience the city as tourists, travelling by train and staying with local friend Thomas for a couple of nights.

The day before the concert, four of us were sightseeing in the city centre when a heavy, lengthy rainstorm sent us to take shelter in a bar for some time where we got fairly drunk and decided to play a game. This involved each of us nominating another to send a fake postcard to a friend of theirs who the writer didn't know, written in the pretence of knowing them, meaning that four people would get a postcard from a total stranger who wrote as if they were old friends.

I can't remember who my victim was, but Thomas wrote a postcard to my friend John claiming he was a former student of John's, who had lost contact and was lamenting how they had fallen out of touch. Poor John was puzzled by this mystery message from a person he couldn't remember at all. Apologies to John – blame the Munich weather and alcohol!

And on the subject of weather – my later third visit to Munich was to prove quite an experience…

30 July 1988: Bremen, Weser-Stadion

After my three-city jaunt to Germany and Switzerland in mid-July, I decided there was a chance to rejoin Margrit (and Vera) via Hamburg for one further show at the end of the month, in Bremen – my 14th and last concert of the 'Tunnel Of Love Express Tour', and an opportunity to visit yet another German city. I remember the tour debut of 'Working On The Highway' (we had heard the tour debut of 'Badlands' at Munich) and an unexpected reference to Nils during 'Sweet Soul Music'.

1988

The *Human Rights Now!* tour

2 September 1988: London, Wembley Stadium

We had no clue at Wembley in June 1988 that Bruce would be back there in September as part of a multi-artist lineup event, 'Human Rights Now!', a global benefit tour for Amnesty International. It felt unprecedented seeing Bruce with other musicians on the same bill, and an official sponsor (Reebok).

There was no question that Bruce and band would headline, after opening the show with a cover of 'Get Up, Stand Up' along with Sting, Peter Gabriel, Tracy Chapman and Youssou N'Dour. Necessarily having a reduced set time, he wisely chose to rock the house with a choice of powerful hits, finishing up with the tour anthem 'Chimes Of Freedom' joined by the others before they all reprised 'Get Up, Stand Up'.

4 September 1988: Paris, Palais Omnisports De Paris-Bercy

After the outdoor experience at London, it was a welcome change to see Bruce and band indoors again for the first time since 1981, at the excellent Bercy arena in Paris. Two shows are always better than one, although we were still adjusting to the unfamiliar multiple bill, here including local musician Michel Jonasz. Bruce's set was similar to London, apart from Sting joining in on 'The River', and the addition of 'Brilliant Disguise', 'Bobby Jean' and 'Raise Your Hand' in place of 'Spare Parts', 'She's The One' and 'Light Of Day'.

Dave, Francoise, and Chantal – Bercy, Paris, 4 September 1988

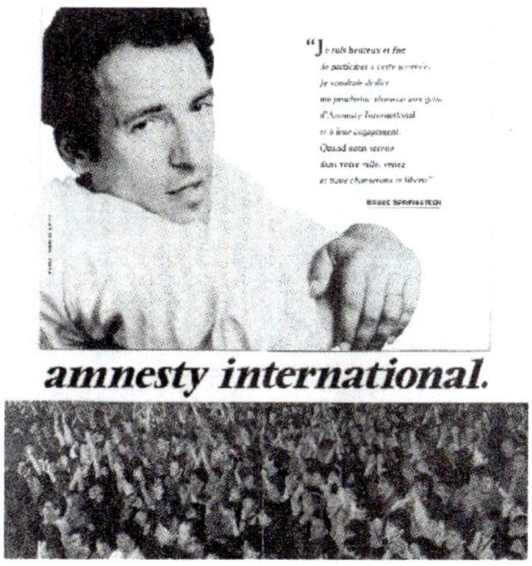

5 September 1988: Paris, Palais Omnisports De Paris-Bercy

A set much the same as the previous night, with the tour premiere of 'Because the Night' replacing 'Bobby Jean'. Whereas London had 'tour passports' (signifying freedom of travel), Paris issued an Amnesty information booklet.

1992-1993

The *1992-1993 World tour*

25 June 1992: Frankfurt, Festhalle

My first shows on the 1992-1993 tour were back at the Festhalle in Frankfurt, where I first caught Bruce in 1981; he referred to his 'River' tour visit when introducing 'Darkness On The Edge Of Town'.

'See you in '93'!

Photo thanks to Marion Mikos

26 June 1992: Frankfurt, Festhalle

As on the previous night, Bruce recognised the presence of local American fans, and spoke a little German while introducing songs. 'The Long Goodbye' was a live premiere; and 'Follow That Dream' was a request from Italian fans. One of the two nights was extremely hot and stuffy in the hall, to the point where I was dehydrating, and by the time 'The River' was played I had to take a break to gulp water from a tap in the toilets – the first time till then I ever deliberately missed a song during a Bruce show.

29 June 1992: Paris, Palais Omnisports de Paris-Bercy

A welcome return to the Bercy arena in Paris for two more June shows before the tour reached London. For 'My Hometown', Bruce joked with the crowd – partly in French – about Babar, the 'famous elephant' popular with his kids.

30 June 1992: Paris, Palais Omnisports de Paris-Bercy

The soundcheck for the second Paris concert featured 'Can't Help Falling In Love' (not played in the show) and 'Rock Ballad', an Elliott Murphy song. Bruce brought Elliott onstage for a unique performance of the song as an encore, introducing him – partly in French – as an old friend from the US, another songwriter who'd also started his career in New York City in the 1970s, and was now a local Paris resident. Elliott would appear alongside Bruce again in future.

6 July 1992: London, Wembley Arena

The London stand of the 1992 tour was five shows at Wembley Arena, back indoors with 'The Other Band' instead of The E Street Band for the only full-band tour until the Reunion era. Springsteen fever still meant major promotional plans such as huge in-store displays at the HMV megastore.

'With Every Wish' returned to the set for four of the five London dates.

HMV store displays in London, July 1992

9 July 1992: London, Wembley Arena

'Real Man' and 'Real World' had their English live debuts at the second Wembley show.

On one of the five dates, 'J.C. Enterprises' artists Chris Hunt and Julian 'Max' Soden brought some of their framed artwork to Wembley.

10 July 1992: London, Wembley Arena

Touring with the still relatively inexperienced 1992-1993 band meant that Bruce had a more limited catalogue which they had all practiced together to draw from to vary his sets, so it was a surprise not only to hear a rare performance of 'Dancing In The Dark', but a solo electric version – he seldom played anything in that style.

12 July 1992: London, Wembley Arena

At the penultimate 1992 London date, Bruce soundchecked Wilson Pickett's 'Ninety-Nine And A Half (Won't Do)', which was not to appear during a set until later that summer. 'The Big Muddy' was played for the first time in England.

A big sign outside Wembley Arena made it clear everyone knew who was doing a major stand there that July.

13 July 1992: London, Wembley Arena

The five-show London run came to an end on 13 July and included 'Prove It All Night' as a tour debut, plus the return of 'Follow That Dream', which had been soundchecked that night in preparation. Very unusually 'Born In The USA' was dropped from the set. Afterwards, a large group of fans gathered at the central Marlborough Hotel, arranged by Badlands.

Fans celebrating at the end of the London stand, Marlborough Hotel; Steve Jump (RIP) seen in the Badlands cap at far right

31 March 1993: Glasgow, Scottish Exhibition + Conference Centre

Glasgow was the start of the 1993 European tour, in the soulless hangar of the SECC. The previous afternoon, a few of us froze outside listening to a lengthy full band rehearsal / soundcheck through the venue doors, including rarities such as 'Point Blank' and 'When You Need Me'. On 31 March, Bruce opened with three solo acoustic songs, as he would do regularly on this tour leg. 'Lucky Town' was filmed live for broadcast on 'Top Of The Pops' the next day. Fittingly, our local 'red-headed woman' friend Alison became Bruce's dance partner on stage during this show.

Mike Wilkinson photo

Alison dancing with Bruce

13 April 1993: Lyon, Halle Tony Garnier

Harry the 'Sole Driver' and I took a road trip to Lyon two days before we were due at Sheffield for a pair of concerts there, as you do. Unfamiliar with the area, we got lost on the outskirts of town and asked a police patrol car for directions. Perhaps with nothing better to do, they indicated we should follow them, and so we had a police escort to the venue, narrowly missing Bruce's own vehicle! Apparently, the building was formerly an abattoir, but luckily no remaining trace of that could be seen.

15 April 1993: Sheffield, Sheffield Arena

Having queued in wintry conditions for tickets outside the arena in early March, we were grateful to be indoors for the two mid-April shows. Bruce's set choices were changing with the new band's increasing confidence, including a gospel-style rendition of Jimmy Cliff's 'Many Rivers To Cross', and the big surprise: a solo acoustic performance of 'Born In The USA' for the first time in Europe.

With Mike and Paul Trimble at Sheffield – photo by Jon Charnley

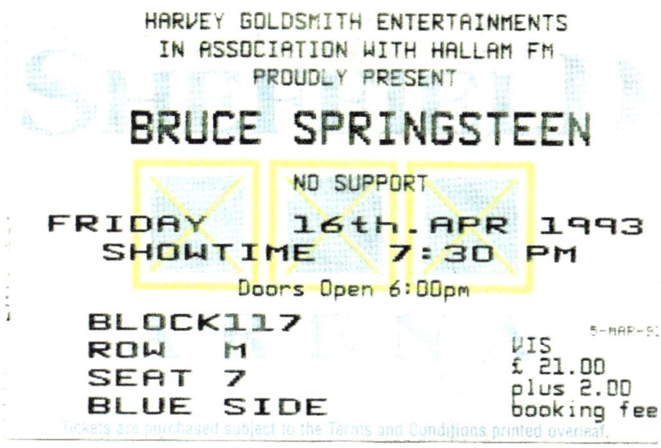

16 April 1993: Sheffield, Sheffield Arena

Highlights of the second night at Sheffield included the tour debut (and a unique performance, by request) of 'Point Blank' which we'd heard being practiced at Glasgow from outside. 'Gloria's Eyes' and 'Soul Driver' made rare appearances too. Making his nightly venture into the crowd during 'Leap Of Faith', someone ripped Bruce's shirt while he was there, causing him to react: 'I feel just like Tom Jones!'

Having collected some discount vouchers somewhere, we ended up enjoying huge amounts of cheap pizza over the two days in Sheffield. Back in London on 17 April, Harry and I took off on yet another (8-day) continental road trip – 'Sole Driver' and 'Sole Passenger' on tour again…

The April 1993 'Sole Driver' / Point Blank road trip to Amsterdam, Rotterdam and Ghent – thanks to Harry Scott for photos and driving!

The April 1993 'Sole Driver' / Point Blank road trip to Amsterdam, Rotterdam and Ghent – thanks to Harry Scott for photos and driving!

The end of the road, back in London - 'skint 'n' blistered'!

19 April 1993: Rotterdam, Sportpaleis Ahoy

Since Bruce first played at the 'Ahoy' in April 1981 during the 'River' tour, I wanted to check out this famous venue, so when two Rotterdam concerts were announced for April 1983, followed by two at Ghent in Belgium, Harry and I reckoned we could combine those four shows with seeing friends along the way.

As he'd been doing in other countries, Bruce continued brief efforts to say something in the local language at these concerts during song introductions, knowing that his words might not sound too authentic, but aware that the idea was appreciated by fans.

While in the Netherlands, we enjoyed exploring Amsterdam, hanging out with our friend Barbara, a US expat there.

Barbara and Harry in Amsterdam

20 April 1993: Rotterdam, Sportpaleis Ahoy

At the second Rotterdam concert, Bruce recognised that many fans there had been at the previous night's show, joking that not everyone could have been there twice, and acknowledging that by switching a few songs around.

Harry and I enjoyed hanging out with friends including Guido and Nick at the show, and afterwards returned to Amsterdam for a long night celebrating with an international bunch of folks: Dutch, Swedish and others. Next stop was across the border into Belgium...

Outside the Ahoy

Post-show drinks in Amsterdam

23 April 1993: Ghent, Flanders Expo

The two concerts in Ghent were Bruce's second appearance in Belgium, after a Brussels show in April 1981. We visited at a time before the introduction of the Euro, when continental countries still had their own local currencies, so we packed both Dutch guilders and Belgian francs for the combined trip.

Again Bruce attempted to speak a little for the locals, and his first idea of Flemish seemed to vary between French and Dutch, and he laughed and said that was all he'd be trying to say for the rest of the night.

24 April 1993: Ghent, Flanders Expo

This was a nervous pre-show time for me, as for some reason I didn't have a ticket in hand in advance unlike at the other concerts, and there was much relief when I finally got hold of my ticket, a higher ticket number than the first night.

A major and welcome surprise was a spontaneous addition of a cover of 'Viva Las Vegas', the first of only two performances in 1993 – and with the theme of luck, I was fortunate enough to catch both of them eventually.

Without realising, the accommodation we'd booked - the Trianon Hotel - also catered for customers wanting rooms by the hour for, er, intimate reasons. There was a clue from the bar menu, notably heavy on champagne and oysters. Our French friend Roger, asking at the Reception if he had a message, got the reply: 'You want a massage?'

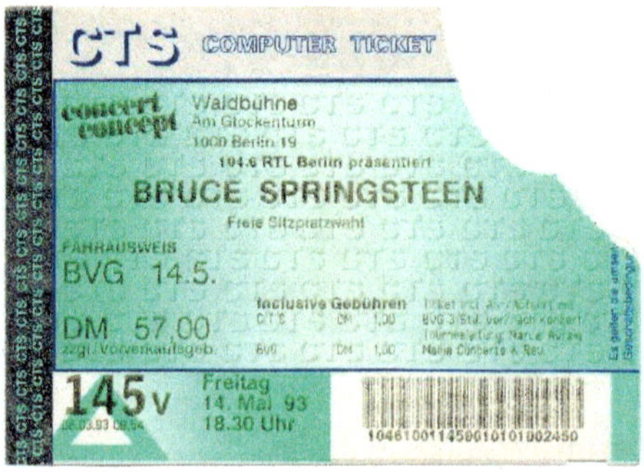

14 May 1993: Berlin, Waldbühne

My 1993 travels resumed in mid-May with my first visit to Berlin, just a few years after the start of German reunification in 1989. After joining Margrit to check out some historic sites including the ICC Halle where Bruce first played in Berlin in 1981, our first open-air concert of the year was at an amphitheatre outside the city, which felt deceptively and pleasantly smaller than its 22,000 capacity.

The first setlist surprise was the extension of the regular opening acoustic trilogy with a fourth song and a live debut, a cover of the country-gospel 'Satan's Jewelled Crown'. Perhaps best known by the Louvin Brothers, this was one of only six times it was played, all in 1993.

An all-time highlight for me was to finally hear a song I'd been chasing since 1988 when I narrowly missed it by one night at New York: 'Across The Borderline', co-written by Ry Cooder, John Hiatt and Jim Dickinson, and its final performance by Bruce until 2012. The previous three performances that month had been in Spain, where Bruce sang the final verse in Spanish, but in Germany the whole song was all in English.

20 May 1993: Dublin, RDS Showjumping Enclosure

From Berlin to Dublin… continuing the mid-90s trend of some of the most colourful ticket designs, often with a photographic element. Having guested with Joe Ely the previous night at the National Stadium, Joe returned the favour at Bruce's show to duet on his own 'Settle For Love'. Having dedicated 'Satan's Jewelled Crown' to 'Jerry', and not content with one special guest, Bruce then introduced Jerry Lee Lewis, who played 'Great Balls Of Fire' and 'Whole Lotta Shakin' Goin' On' – his first of only two Springsteen appearances. Hilariously, advertising for Jerry Lee Lewis soon afterwards used the description 'fresh from his world tour with Bruce Springsteen'!

22 May 1993: Milton Keynes, The National Bowl

Bizarrely, early posters for the Milton Keynes concert described it as Bruce's 'only UK show' (ignoring Glasgow and Sheffield), later corrected to 'final UK show' for the 1993 tour. About a third of the show was professionally filmed for an abandoned TV special, along with the 28 May concert in Stockholm, although the footage circulated among fans as 'The Lost TV Special'. This show featured the second (and final) appearance of 'Viva Las Vegas', a much repeated audience request that day. Curiously, the soundcheck included 'Great Balls Of Fire', as in Jerry Lee Lewis was expected to guest again; and a mysterious, unknown country-style tune. Two days later in west London, Bruce unexpectedly sang a karaoke version of 'Jumpin' Jack Flash' at The Stanhope Arms – his really final UK performance that year. (I was at The Marlborough Hotel and the Old Orleans restaurant then, along with other blissfully unaware friends.)

Friends in London NOT at The Stanhope Arms where Bruce was…

1996-1997

The *Ghost Of Tom Joad* tour

17 February 1996: Hamburg, Congress Centrum

In 1981, Bruce opened his European tour at Hamburg and four shows later I caught his fourth continental show, at Frankfurt; in 1996 I did the same with the geography reversed, starting with the fourth show again – at Hamburg instead of Frankfurt this time.

Bruce remembered (or had been reminded of) the significance of Hamburg 1981, but made a point of his 'disclaimer' that he urged people to monitor their neighbours: 'politely ask them to shut the fuck up'. The tour was already abbreviated as The STFU Tour. It was quite an educational experience for us longtime fans who were always used to expressing ourselves at Springsteen concerts, and I can vividly remember actually sitting on my hands during the songs that first time, in case I inadvertently felt moved to clap, and also a sense of really focusing as the performance volume wasn't what we were used to, and I didn't want to miss a thing, both Bruce's solo acoustic playing and his often lengthy spoken introductions. Years later the same effect would occur both during the 'Devils & Dust' tour shows and especially at 'Springsteen On Broadway'.

I kept diary notes at the time, with the heading 'From German town yeah we did ride', also noting the relatively short set times of around two and a quarter hours:

Sitting a fair way back, I could still see Bruce walking on in semi-darkness, and then he went straight into 'The Ghost Of Tom Joad'. I felt like it cut through me immediately and I just sat, pierced, my attention totally commanded even at some distance, and so it continued, especially for the quietest songs where it seemed I hardly breathed, and I wasn't alone.

Some people's idea of an acoustic evening is that they'd be bored with two hours of one musician with just a guitar and harmonica to accompany his voice, and as if to challenge this right away, Bruce powered into 'Adam Raised A Cain', showing just how much variety you can get out of an acoustic guitar, and transforming the song yet again from the earlier solo arrangement from 1993. 'Straight Time' and 'Highway 29' both took on new life beyond the studio versions, as I guessed they would. The latter is remarkable partly due to a ghostly keyboard being played offstage (by technician Kevin Buell). As always with a Springsteen show, a point comes several songs in when the ice is truly broken – on this tour, it's with 'Darkness On The Edge Of Town', given extraordinary urgency and strength, for me better than any previous version – causing shivers up the spine, and a fresh surge of adrenalin. When you think it's hard for Bruce to top that, you get 'Murder Incorporated' with its slow anger, and marvel how he doesn't break strings with every blow.

Maybe sensing that we need a moment to recover, Bruce followed with only the fifth 'Nebraska' song I'd experienced live, 'Mansion On The Hill', keeping it simple, straight and close to the original, which worked perfectly. He took me by surprise next with 'Dead Man Walkin'', coming earlier than I expected, and casually referring to the movie afterwards (now his second Oscar-nominated song). 'Sell It And They Will Come', a modern-day Guthrie-style protest song, was prefaced by an attempt to describe to a European audience the 'infomercials' on American TV – this year's follow-up to '57 Channels' in a way. Bruce jokingly underlined their crassness by referring to his 'sexual fantasies' being the context in which he wrote the song. After this mid-point of levity, he started a two-part Vietnam veterans saga with 'Brothers Under The Bridge', which would have fitted perfectly on the new album, the second part – of course – being the redefined blues of 'Born In The USA', retaining all the anger and removing all the anthem from the song. 'Dry Lightning' stays pretty faithful to the album version, striking home poignantly with a picture of just missing someone.

Another surprise for me followed with 'Reason To Believe', opening with a soft whining (almost like an acoustic intro to 'Backstreets'), suddenly stepping up a gear into a 'State Trooper'/'Spare Parts' rhythm – I found this gave it a new urgency, combined with vocals of suppressed hysteria. 'Youngstown', pared down from the album arrangement, is quietly solemn but strikes to the heart, setting the mood for the next four songs, done seated. 'Sinaloa Cowboys', 'The Line' and 'Balboa Park' belong together in that sequence and create a vivid portrait of the life of Mexican immigrants. The trilogy is capped by the set-closer 'Across The Border', bringing hope and optimism, and again featuring Kevin on the off-stage keyboards.

Back on his feet for the encores, Bruce heartily sent out 'Does This Bus Stop At 82nd Street', complete with brief Dylan parody, the first time I'd seen this and a real joy as a result. 'This Hard Land' continued the upbeat mood before he returned again with an understated 'Streets Of Philadelphia', almost falteringly brief despite (or because of?) a rapturous welcome and people waving lighters in the darkened hall. 'Galveston Bay' wrapped up the story-songs from the new album, and I fully expected 'My Best Was Never Good Enough' to be the last song, as the lights came up and Bruce seemed to wave a definite farewell afterwards. Suddenly he ran back on, grabbed a guitar and treated us to 'The Promised Land' which I'd never had as an acoustic version – a fitting closer.

18 February 1996: Düsseldorf, Philipshalle

Mike had joined me to team up with Margrit for her hometown show in Hamburg, and we all continued to Düsseldorf for the next show the following day. The solo acoustic format (and the season) meant we were indoors this tour, which has always been a preference since starting that way in 1981. Being our initial shows on this tour, we were still experiencing some new songs for the first time, or the first time as acoustic arrangements, with a few variations in the setlists.

My notes from the time:

Düsseldorf, while lacking the novelty of a first show, repeated my 1981 German experience of just getting into the venue in time after a long drive. More of a shed than a theatre, a closer seat in this larger hall really made a difference as Bruce's expressions were visible and the sense of intimacy greater. The set's structure was mostly similar to Hamburg, but with the welcome appearance of 'Nebraska' (making it the seventh song from the album for me) in place of 'Mansion On The Hill', and omitting 'Dead Man Walkin''. Bruce managed to stifle an isolated attempt at clapping during 'Nebraska' by slowing it down abruptly. Instead of 'The Promised Land' at the end, he played 'No Surrender' before 'My Best Was Never Good Enough', speeding it up from the usual live rendition.

28 February 1996: Manchester, Apollo Theatre

Bruce's 1996 UK leg was 12 shows in seven cities over three months, his most extensive British visit since 1981. As I wrote at the time:

The echoes of the 1981 tour continued as the first British leg began in Manchester – especially as the Apollo had been the site of one of the first English shows then. The mostly northern audience gave Bruce a rousing welcome, and he responded with set variations such as 'Johnny 99' (superior to the standard version from 1985), given a fresh, fast treatment that fitted neatly after 'Darkness On The Edge Of Town'. 'Spare Parts' took the place of 'Reason To Believe', with a similar arrangement and intensity. Trying to guess which songs Bruce maybe couldn't do in the solo acoustic format, I'd listed 'Bobby Jean'. Wrong! Replacing 'Does This Bus Stop At 82nd Street', it worked with surprising poignancy as the first encore. The real jaw-dropper was the final number, when 'My Best Was Never Good Enough' was dropped in favour of an astonishing new re-working of 'The Promised Land'. Bruce simply slapped the strings and tapped the guitar body, singing meanwhile with extraordinary intensity and a falsetto howl like nothing we'd heard from him before. It felt like the whole theatre held its collective breath, and then thundered approval as he raised the guitar and took his bows. Worth the price of admission alone.

29 February 1996: Birmingham, Symphony Hall

Friends joining in for this rare 'leap day' Bruce show included Chris Hunt, and from the US, Holly Cara Price, who accompanied us for the week. Curiously, 'Lucky Town' was an encore option on the setlist, dropped in favour of 'Does This Bus Stop At 82nd Street'.

My 1996 diary notes:

Unlike the other three regional shows of this section of the UK tour, the Birmingham concert took place in a venue not played in 1981, the relatively new Symphony Hall. It was a stunning setting, and Bruce remarked on its beauty and the hush it inspired in the crowd that night (to be repeated later at the Royal Albert Hall in April). 'Dead Man Walkin'' made a rare re-appearance, and he offered us the choice between a song about sex or one about TV shopping – namely, 'It's The Little Things That Count' versus 'Sell It And They Will Come'. 'Sell It…' won the vote, prompting a wry comment from Bruce about the state of sexual interest in Birmingham! Afterwards, a call from one fan: 'can we have the sex one now?' brought a simple 'OK', and the song in question.

2 March 1996: Newcastle, City Hall

Holly was desperate to exchange tickets with me as I had a much closer seat, so this 'behind mixer' seat is her original. As I wrote in 1996:

The smallest venue on the British leg, the City Hall was the site of the first UK show in 1981, and Bruce remembered its intimacy. Again, we had both 'Sell It And They Will Come' and 'It's The Little Things That Count', this time the latter being introduced with a shortened version of the opening story; Bruce may have been briefly distracted by the heartfelt yell from one fan: 'Oh Bruce! I fookin' looove ya, man!' Bruce smiled in reply: 'I guess he just had to say that.' The shouter than called out that he'd see him in London, to which Bruce responded: 'How will I know you?'

3 March 1996: Edinburgh, Playhouse

We stayed with Harry's parents in Fife, and his dad reassured Mike: 'I gave up killing Englishmen a few years ago!' Apparently the soundcheck included about five songs, and Bruce admired the stage design for 'The Phantom Of The Opera' musical under which he played. My 1996 notes:

Another small theatre from the 1981 tour marked Bruce's only Scottish appearance this time, and he commented on the enormous props from 'The Phantom Of The Opera' overshadowing him. One of the biggest surprises this month came when instead of either of the two new story-songs normally opted between, Bruce announced a real rarity, only done a couple of times previously – the European debut of 'The Wish', introduced with observations about nations that qualified as 'mother-lovers' – adding that he'd seen people so drunk in Edinburgh that the only people they could go home to were their mothers!

17 March 1996: Dublin, The Mean Fiddler (Joe Ely gig)

1996 diary:

It seemed absurd, even for a veteran fan like myself. Having seen Joe Ely's two excellent gigs in London the week before, we heard from Terry Clarke, his support, that Joe's final European show in Dublin at the Mean Fiddler that Sunday was rumoured to feature a special guest – and Harry only heard it because we stayed for a final drink at the end of the show instead of going straight home. The absurdity was that we'd already booked flights for Bruce's two official Irish shows on Tuesday and Wednesday at Belfast and Dublin – and I couldn't take more than the three days off work (Thursday was reserved for travelling back and a Joe Grushecky gig at The Borderline). It would mean travelling to Dublin once on Sunday, returning at the crack of dawn to work on Monday, and flying back to Ireland on Tuesday. After spending Saturday in extremes of denial and decisiveness (I can't go! – I must go! – I can't go! etc), on Sunday morning I rang

Ryanair and stretched the credit card once more. I was going. I must be mad, but it felt like it had to be done. Mike went through a similar dilemma of indecision, but I left him with my travel details, and eventually he turned up in Ireland an hour or two after me!

Dublin, early evening, St Patrick's Day. Dreading that the show would be sold out simply because folks would be looking for any kind of party in the city that night, but we got in line and bought tickets easily on the door, and took up position at the front left of the high stage. Terry Clarke played his now familiar enjoyable set, seemingly dropping a hint of the treat to come during 'Hometown' when he changed the words to refer to a lot of hearts being broken in his hometown when Bruce Springsteen got married. The first real heartstopper came when Bruce's minder Terry Magovern appeared from behind the backstage curtain and studied the crowd. Even then it was hard to believe it could really be happening. During Joe's set, I wondered if it was just my imagination that there could be an air of expectancy even onstage – or was it just the atmosphere of the end of his tour in this musical city on a celebrated night? It struck me that certain songs we'd previously heard early in the set - which we associated with Bruce - might be being saved for later, like 'All Just To Get To You' and 'Settle For Love'.

Then it happened. Joe spoke of being glad to share the final night with us, and also glad to share it with 'my friend Bruce'. As the screams and yells erupted, and we knew who would appear, it still took a moment to register until the curtain moved and that familiar guy walked on – dressed for rock'n'roll instead of an acoustic gig, with silver-tipped boots and a chunky chain hanging in his back pocket, his normally slicked-back hair loose. He strapped on a spare electric guitar for the first time in months and stood between Joe and Jesse 'Guitar' Taylor, grinning at Joe for the cue to 'All Just To Get To You'. No song could have felt more appropriate for the circumstances. Just then, it was all worthwhile.

My only previous experience of Bruce in a club had been with Cats On A Smooth Surface in 1982, when he undisputably led the bar band and took total control of the show. Now, 14 years later, the contrast was fascinating. It was immediately apparent that Bruce consciously assumed the role of guest guitarist and that it was still Joe's gig, constantly hanging back slightly and watching the bandleader for the nod to step forward and solo – for example in 'Oh Boy', where he managed to retain this restraint while delivering some serious trademark guitar. Without his own microphone, he was often leaning forward to share Joe's (causing a frenzy of flashbulb-popping) and again, the sense of holding back merged with his unmistakable energy and charisma on stage. Much credit to Joe and his band that it felt a team effort. 'Settle For Love' called for a hearty singalong from the crowd, and as they went off afterwards it could have been over – I imagined that if the band might come back for another encore (without Bruce) of 'I'm A Thousand Miles From Home' that he could still wander on in time to join in on the choruses, as on the record.

A brief encore break, and Bruce was immediately back on again with the band for a medley of 'Fingernails' (a favourite of mine, one I thought they wouldn't do without piano) with the segments Joe and Bruce had played together in Dublin in 1993, 'Buddy Brown' and 'Matchbox'. Then Bruce obviously had an idea and whispered in Joe's ear; he nodded, and Bruce led the band into 'Long Tall Sally'.

The band went off once more, and that could have been it again, but the audience was thunderous, and there was one song left we knew they'd done together twice before, and Joe and Bruce came back on their own to cover Woody Guthrie's 'Blowin' Down That Old Dusty Road'. Typically, Bruce had trouble with the acoustic guitar, Joe's own (complete with JE on the strap), grinning sheepishly as he was helped to get it ready. Once again, for a duet of equals, he balanced both restraint and dominance, stepping back to let Joe sing and then leading the way to change the intensity of the song, but never overshadowing his partner.

Harry had been shooting pictures. I had one frame of colour film left on my old camera; Harry took it from me, carefully composed a shot, and snapped a perfect souvenir.

Throughout the set, Bruce seemed happy and relaxed, in his element, immensely enjoying a night off playing covers with a respected friend. Then it was properly over, and he laughed as he pressed the plectrum into one fan's hand, waved, and they were all off. It was time for us to celebrate with each other, dance, drink and compare notes on the experience. For me, the delight was not only that I'd finally seen another club appearance, but that I'd been able to share it with friends on European turf. The week had just begun – it was going to be a long, strange one – but totally worth it, all just to get to him.

Joe Ely & Bruce, Dublin 1996 - photos thanks to Harry Scott

19 March 1996: Belfast, King's Hall

Thanks to our Irish friend Paul, Mike and I got tickets for both the Belfast and Dublin shows in 1996. Like for Bruce, it was our first visit to Northern Ireland. Paul also managed to get into the hall early and listen to Bruce's soundcheck, about 45 minutes of partial songs, all played in the set. I spotted the concession staff had branded t-shirts unusually combining Bruce's name with the Coca-Cola sponsor, and bought one from a staff member after the show. The concert was later released as part of the Nugs live archive series. I made notes from the trip:

Two days later, we were back in Dublin and en route by train to Belfast. Bruce's Northern Ireland debut seemed like an essential show to attend, and he was conscious it had taken him awhile to visit when he addressed the King's Hall: 'Glad to finally be here'. The line in 'The Ghost Of Tom Joad' about 'somebody struggling to be free' brought a whoop of recognition from the floor, and given Irish history, adding a dimension previously not so keenly felt to the song that night. Bruce responded again before 'Bobby Jean', saying that he 'shoulda come sooner', and later expressing a hope for the possibility of establishing 'some kind of community – I wish you peace.'

20 March 1996: Dublin, The Point Theatre

As I wrote at the time:

The Point Depot on the outskirts of Dublin made for an interesting venue, an ultra-modern converted warehouse (complete with escalators) by the river, and possibly one of the only Springsteen concerts accessible by boat! An enterprising ferry company shuttled fans cheaply to and from the location and the centre of town. 'Mansion On The Hill' sounded appropriately ironic that night in that building. Despite rumours of guest appearances from the likes of locals like U2, Bruce held his ground on his own, but no less effectively.

16 April 1996: London, Royal Albert Hall

Rescheduled from 22 March due to Bruce attending the Academy Awards to sing 'Dead Man Walkin''. Before the first three London shows actually went on sale, a group of us went on a tip-off to the Royal Albert Hall and queued overnight for tickets, only to find it was a false alarm – we treated it as a dry run, and on 29 January successfully got our tickets the same way. Thanks to Mike for my ticket here. My 1996 notes:

Bruce returned to London for the first time since 1992 for a season of six shows at both the Royal Albert Hall and Brixton Academy. He was moved to remark on the beauty of the building at the Albert Hall, and by all accounts overcame its notorious sound quality variations in the upper levels. As if to mischievously stir up the somewhat sedate first night crowd, particularly the inevitable VIPs and industry guests, he debuted an unreleased song about 'a go-go bar at Christmas time'. Finally I had my wish of a Christmas song in the UK – although not the one I expected! Apparently titled 'Pilgrim In The Temple Of Love', the song was actually referred to by Bruce later a couple of times as 'Santa Gets A Blow-job' – and as such it's destined to be nicknamed, as that's the heart of the tale! A surprise set positioning followed immediately, the UK premiere of 'My Best Was Never Good Enough', more effective at that point than in its usual encore slot. 'No Surrender' came with the exhortation to sing along – the first time I'd heard Bruce actively encourage audience participation on this tour.

17 April 1996: London, Royal Albert Hall

Rescheduled from 27 March. The English live debut of 'The Wish', which had first been played in the UK in Edinburgh the previous month.

Always a familiar and welcome sight at Bruce shows: Edwin Shirley Trucking vehicles, whose logo appropriately doubles as 'E ST'

22 April 1996: London, Royal Albert Hall

The third London show was one of three added later, including two at Brixton Academy, making six in all, so these tickets reflected the correct date. Thanks to Scott for this one. A night that will always be remembered by those lucky enough to be there as the European live debut (and first major public performance, if you don't count a couple of low-key airings in 1972) of 'The Angel', which would only appear once more, in 2009. I was sitting with Magda, and we just gaped at each other once we recognised the lyrics. Eternal thanks to Martin for managing to request the song, as he documented for Badlands! It was also the European debut of 'Blinded By The Light'. Writing at the time, I recalled:

A stunning first took everyone by surprise after 'Sell It And They Will Come' on the 22nd – no less than 'The Angel', which Bruce introduced misleadingly by saying he hadn't done it since 1974 – we were racking our brains, as it's generally held that it's never really been done live! Like many musicians, he has a hazy memory of dates at times. Whatever, an absolute treat, straight and simple. Apparently relaxed enough to try other rarities on this multi-night stand, Bruce also gave us 'Blinded By The light' as first encore – a classic performance because not only did he have to change guitars mid-song (something I'd seen him do more easily with a band, but never solo!) but had to finish the song in a different key to match the second guitar's tuning – sheer professionalism!

why did bruce play the *Angel*?

by martin stern

I have never been particulary interested in meeting the man whose career I have followed for 15 years. Seeing the shows and collecting poor audience tapes (only to agonise over which to erase) has always been sufficient. For many years I have followed Bruce's own advice and trusted the music, not the man.

It was sheer chance that led me into the soundcheck before the 22nd April show at the Albert Hall. That evening I arrived far too early and wandered into the building at about 6.00pm, intending no more than to get a table in the restaurant so that my friends and I could enjoy a pre-show supper and debate over the likely set list. (Although these days, we are just as likely to end up discussing babies and house hunting!)

On the upper levels of the hall, the soundcheck could be heard clearly and after pushing through two sets of doors, I found myself in the Choir section behind the stage. I settled into the far corner, hoping to eavesdrop and expecting to be thrown out almost immediately. My presence was acknowledged by the crew but for some reason I was allowed to stay.

bruce worked his way through several songs from the set, with the addition of 'My Father's House', his road crew ensuring that the autocue scrolled correctly to any song that took his fancy. Bruce seemed very relaxed and after each song thanked the 'audience'. His light mood encouraged me to request a song. I took the view that there was no point in asking for anything obscure and so I requested 'If I Should Fall Behind', in the knowledge that it had already been performed on the tour. To my surprise Bruce held a mock conference with a roadie and announced to the unseen fan that it would be no problem.

By now I was gaining in confidence. I said that I had only asked for that song as he would be unlikely to play 'The Angel'. I suppose that this was more a dare than a request. Bruce immediately strummed a few chords. The 'big book' appeared on a lectern and Bruce performed the song, finishing with a 'There you go buddy'. I thanked him and mumbled that it was underrated (maybe a small exaggeration!). He later ran through the song once more, the big book again being set up by an attentive roadie. He then commented, possibly tongue in cheek, that perhaps the song should have been on the new album.

I had a sneaking feeling that Bruce was in the mood to perform that song that night. As he began 'The Angel' for the first time ever in concert I could almost hear the sound of jaws dropping in disbelief. It amuses to think of fans all around the world wondering what the hell was going on that night.

I still don't feel that I have met Bruce, after all to him I was just a voice coming from the gloom. However, I hope that I may have influenced the tour, as from that night he seemed to enjoy weaving older material into the show. Later in the week I played the original version of the song to my wife. Interestingly, her reaction was almost identical to Bruce's comment after he had performed it – 'What's is he going on about?'

Martin's story about requesting 'The Angel' featured by Badlands

24 April 1996: London, Brixton Academy

Unusually, for two of his four April shows in London, Bruce switched venues – from the Royal Albert Hall to Brixton Academy. 1996 was the only time he played there. Having soundchecked both 'Atlantic City' and 'Red Headed Woman' previously at the Royal Albert Hall, we had their tour debuts, also the European debut of the latter, with a new verse. Also the tour debut and only tour performance of 'Seeds', and another European debut – the rare 'State Trooper'. My 1996 diary noted:

Brixton Academy immediately felt less formal than the RAH, and Bruce's first night there soon proved a real shake-up of the setlist, including 'Atlantic City' (displacing 'Adam Raised A Cain' for the first time on the tour), 'State Trooper' (my eighth 'Nebraska' song now), 'Red Headed Woman' and 'Seeds'.

25 April 1996: London, Brixton Academy

The second Brixton continued with changes, including the tour debut of 'Highway Patrolman', and unusually, guests: Elliott Murphy and Joe Grushecky (in town for their own show) joined in for the English debut of 'Blowin' Down That Old Dusty Road'. Introducing 'Atlantic City', Bruce added to his usual call for quiet ('If you feel like cheering me on during a song, I've done some drugs and I'm feeling mighty confident so I really don't need it') a plea to put away flash cameras, joking he'd had to come out and take names previously. 'If I Should Fall Behind' was a request for 'Malcolm and Brenda', and 'Point Blank' was a spontaneous reaction to a call for it from the balcony. I noted then:

Delighted at the vocal response from his 'younger fans', Bruce dedicated 'No Surrender' to them. Seen approaching the hall before the show, Joe Grushecky and Elliott Murphy joined Bruce onstage for an extra and final encore, 'Old Dusty Road' (coincidentally done with Joe Ely at the only other guest appearance at one of Bruce's shows this tour, at Austin).

27 April 1996: London, Royal Albert Hall

Another rescheduled date from March, but my ticket has the April date. Returning for his final London night to the Royal Albert Hall, Bruce played the only tour performance (and European debut) of 'Pony Boy' first, curiously displacing 'The Ghost Of Tom Joad' in that opening slot for the first time on the tour. Encouraged by recent set variations, I joined in the requests…

Having faxed a request for 'I Wish I Were Blind' (from my wish list) to the Albert Hall, my hopes were raised when I was told it had been rehearsed at the soundcheck, but that was to be its only performance of the final night, my 83rd Springsteen show and 15th of this tour. 'Pony Boy' took us all by surprise as the very first song, preceding 'The Ghost Of Tom Joad' for the first time on the tour. Since 'Atlantic City' now assumed the old 'Adam Raised A Cain' place, a request for this song about Bruce's father followed his maternal reminiscences of 'The Wish'. We got the sense that Bruce had been about to spring another new one after that, as there was much guitar-changing and indecision. 'Point Blank' made another appearance, as did 'Blinded By The Light', Bruce this time determined to get it right, and more or less succeeding.

Bruce Springsteen Re-Schedules London Shows

Academy Nominates Bruce Springsteen For An Oscar

Bruce Springsteen has been nominated for an Oscar from the film "Dead Man Walking." He has therefore been asked to perform at the Oscar ceremony on Monday 25 March 1996.

This will result in Bruce postponing his London concerts at the Royal Albert Hall. These dates are being rescheduled as follows:

Ticket Holders For:	New Date:
Friday 22 March	Tuesday 16 April
Saturday 23 March	Saturday 27 April
Wednesday 27 March	Wednesday 17 April

Ticketholders should keep their tickets as they will *only* be valid for the new date.

Any ticket holder unable to attend must return their ticket to point of purchase for a refund. Refunds will only be accepted until Friday 8 March.

As a result of these changes, Brcue has agreed to perform extra shows. These are as follows:

Monday 22 April - Royal Albert Hall
Ticket Price: 25 pounds

Wednesday 24 April - Brixton Academy
Thursday 25 April - Brixton Academy
Ticket Price: 25 pounds
The Brixton Academy shows will be *all seated*.

Tickets will go on sale at 9:00 AM on Wednesday 28 February *for telephone sales only*, no personal callers, from the following numbers:
Royal Albert Hall (22 April) 0171 589 8212 or 0171 420 1000
Brixton Academy (24/25 April) 0171 924 9999 or 0171 403 3331
Maximum two tickets per person.

Please note that the following concert dates will go ahead as scheduled
[Manchester, Birmingham, Newcastle, Edinburgh]

end of press release.

Press release on the re-scheduling of the 1996 London shows

25 May 1997: Paris, Palais Des Congrès De Paris

Unexpectedly, presumably because he was enjoying the solo acoustic tour so much, Bruce extended the 'Ghost Of Tom Joad' tour with another final swing around continental Europe in 1997. Mike and I decided to catch the last two shows, as Paris seemed so close to London by Eurostar (Mike had recently returned from seeing Bruce in Warsaw with Harry). The French promoter was emphatic in the billing of the solo acoustic tour as such, with a local poster stressing: 'only with his guitar and his harmonica'. By this time things had evolved and Bruce was even looser and more encouraging with audience participation, particularly on the encores. He was extending 'No Surrender' with a longer guitar introduction, and 'Long Time Comin'' and 'Growin' Up' were new to me this tour.

26 May 1997: Paris, Palais Des Congrès De Paris

Bruce finally wrapped up the 'Ghost Of Tom Joad' tour, which had started two years ago in 1995. Local US expatriate and friend Elliott Murphy joined Bruce to guest on two encores, a unique Springsteen performance of 'Diamonds By The Yard' and the first time in France for 'Blowin' Down That Old Dusty Road'. 'For You' was played for only the fourth time on the tour. By this stage, tech Kevin Buell was getting a humorous mention from Bruce before 'Sinaloa Cowboys' as 'mystery keyboardist' as well as for various bizarre types of assistance.

1999-2000

The *Reunion* tour

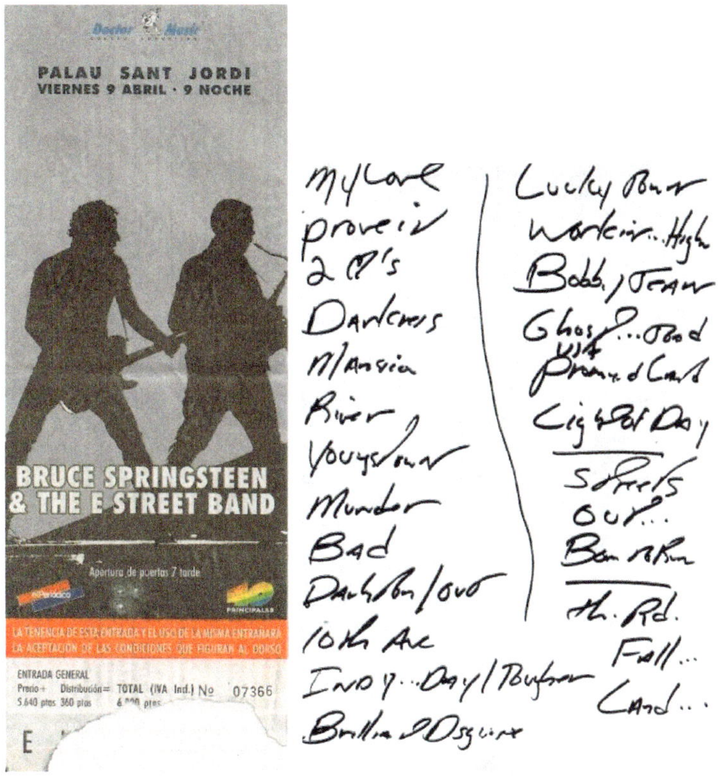

9 April 1999: Barcelona, Palau Sant Jordi

The reunion tour began in Spain with two indoor arena shows by the newly expanded E Street Band, Stevie Van Zandt having returned, and their first official appearance since 1988. Bruce made a point about both a rebirth and rededication of the band, highlighting this with multiple vocal contributions during 'If I Should Fall Behind', and the tour's theme song, 'Land Of Hope And Dreams'. A few of my friends planned a group trip from the UK, and having just started a new job, it took some negotiation for me to take time off so soon, my boss keeping me until the last minute before I had to rush for my plane to catch the others up. Thanks always to Sal for organising and distributing our tickets.

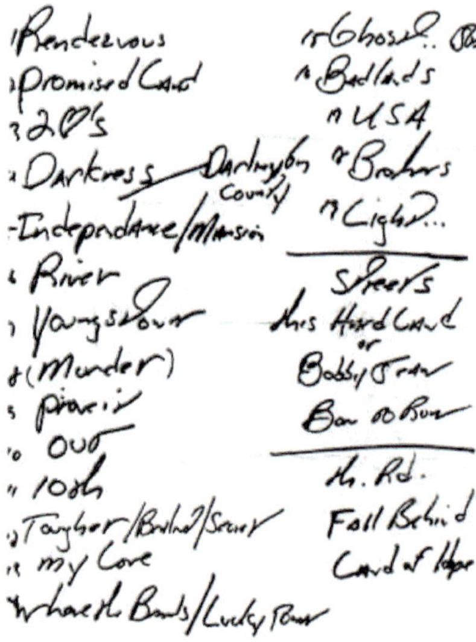

11 April 1999: Barcelona, Palau Sant Jordi

The soundcheck for the second night at Barcelona intriguingly included 'I Wanna Be With You, 'Factory', 'Nebraska' and a very rare 'Secret Garden' – none of which were played that night. We did get 'Rendezvous', 'Independence Day', 'Brothers Under The Bridge' and a unique arrangement of 'Born In The USA', which started off acoustically before the full band version took over. The changes made for an optimistically promising start to the tour, and the overall impression was that it was just so great to see Bruce, Stevie and all the band back together again at last for a new era.

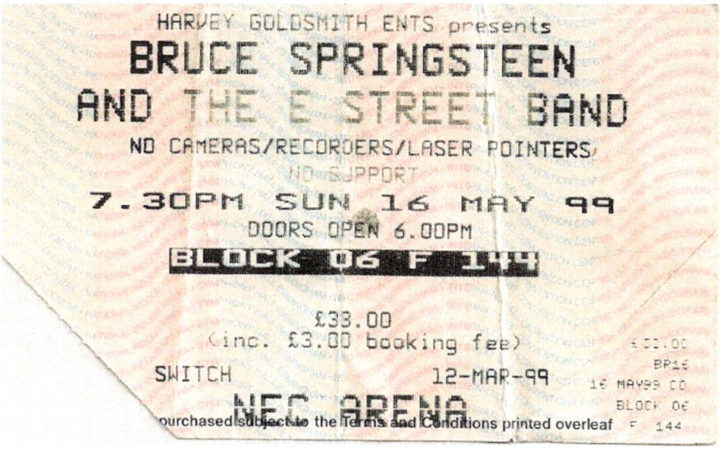

16 May 1999: Birmingham, NEC Arena

After the two Barcelona shows, my next dates would have been the two concerts at Manchester in early May, but I was at a wedding of a good friend in the Netherlands, and so Manchester 1999 is a rare example of missed UK mainland shows for me since 1981.

Returning to the same indoor arena at which he'd finished the 1981 UK tour, Bruce reverted to the more familiar fully acoustic arrangement of 'Born In The USA', as he had done at Manchester. 'War' featured local guest Edwin Starr, as in 1988; an exclusive on the 1999-2000 tour for Birmingham. The third of four shows to date at this Midlands building.

Having completed three UK shows, next was a stand of four London shows at Earls Court, the first and only time Bruce played that arena, although it was previously rumoured for the 1985 tour before the success of 'Born In The USA' meant they needed to switch to outdoor stadiums. Despite the notoriously poor acoustics at Earls Court, it was still a relief to be indoors and have more shows due to the smaller capacity there than if it had been stadiums.

18 May 1999: London, Earls Court

Bruce and the band did extensive soundchecks for each of the four nights at Earls Court. Part of the first night's soundcheck was filmed and confirmed that 'Racing In The Street' was included, although not played in the set. On one night, 'As Long As I (Can Be With You)' was rehearsed. 'Jungleland' seems to have been a request, if not already on the planned setlist.

Thanks to 'Mr A Scott' for this ticket.

19 May 1999: London, Earls Court

Thanks to Mike for my second night ticket, the longest set of the stand, with seven encores. Curiously, the Earls Court tickets appeared to indicate sponsorship (by P&O), not something usually permitted in Bruce's contracts. 'Glory Days' was soundchecked, but not played in London this tour.

Typically for a stand at London, friends came from all over, and we had a large international gathering at Maxwell's restaurant in Covent Garden one day in May around the shows.

21 May 1999: London, Earls Court

Another long soundcheck, including 'My Hometown' and 'Loose Ends'. A surprise opener instead of 'My Love Will Not Let You Down' was 'I Wanna Be With You', its first appearance in England. 'You Can Look (But You Better Not Touch)' was a tour debut, as was 'Meeting Across The River' (preceding 'Jungleland') – getting its first live airing since the end of the 'Darkness On The Edge Of Town' tour in 1979.

One of the hazards of the venue was its folding seats, as unfortunate (inebriated?) audience members behind us discovered to their cost, and our distraction – and chose 'Meeting Across The River', of all songs to do so. They bought beers and placed them on a folding chair, but as drinks were lifted off the chair, the reducing weight caused the chair springs to flip the chair up – and beer went everywhere, including down the backs of our seats, bags etc. Not the memory of the show we expected, for sure!

23 May 1999: London, Earls Court

Although this and the previous ticket show the price as zero, I'm sure I paid the usual £35 for both! Bruce brought his London stand to an end with the fourth show at Earls Court, featuring another lengthy and interesting soundcheck which included a rare 'Blinded By The Light', 'Give The Girl A Kiss'. 'Ramrod', 'Roulette' and 'Red Headed Woman' – only the final song appearing in the set, in part, during 'Tenth Avenue Freeze-Out'. Despite rehearsing the full band intro to 'Born In The USA', Bruce played the full acoustic version during the show.

29 May 1999: Berlin, Parkbühne Wuhlheide

I decided to wrap up my travels on the 1999 tour with a visit with Mike to Berlin for two open-air concerts over the bank holiday weekend. A lengthy power cut at Heathrow airport meant major take-off delays even after we had boarded. We landed around midnight, too late to make our hotel reservation across town nearer the venue, and got a taxi to take us to the nearest alternative hotel – a couple of minutes away. By the time I called my wife at home (no mobiles), she'd been panicking as she'd called the original hotel and they had no idea where I was; I hadn't checked in there. Mike recalled:

'Dan and I flew to Berlin, but not before technical problems at Heathrow had kept us on the ground, in our seats, for five hours. They even served our in-flight meals on the ground. When we landed in Berlin, we'd been on the plane for seven hours, long enough to fly to New York. The gigs took place in an outdoor amphitheatre with less capacity than Earls Court in London, where Bruce had just played four nights. To get to the venue, we took a train into what used to be East Berlin, a journey that would have been impossible only a decade before. A great trip, full of music and history.'

30 May 1999: Berlin, Parkbühne Wuhlheide

One of the few advantages of an open-air show is that it's often easier to hear the soundcheck from outside, and I was fascinated to make out 'Trouble River' among the somewhat muffled sound of a few songs that day.

Although 'Independence Day' was also soundchecked and apparently on the setlist, it wasn't played. 'I Wanna Be With You' was a welcome rare opener, as it was on 21 May in London.

At one of the two Berlin shows, we arrived at the venue to find a long line of fans waiting to go in, and greeted our old friend Ralf standing near the front of the queue. After a brief chat, we said we'd better go and get places at the back of the line before it got much longer. Ralf invited us to join him where he was, but that felt awkward: wouldn't the people behind him mind if we did that? Ralf replied: 'It's no problem, they're with me!' And thus reassured, we took up his kind suggestion. Thanks, Berlin!

26 June 2000: New York City, Madison Square Garden

I made it to the last four concerts of Bruce's 10-night stand closing the Reunion tour at Madison Square Garden in NYC. That night, a promotional video for 'American Skin (41 Shots)' was filmed during the soundcheck, which also notably included 'Real World' and 'The Promise'.

Bruce opened the show with 'Another Thin Line', co-written with Joe Grushecky, and he referred to it again before 'Born In the USA', making his regular call for support for the local hunger campaign organisation, the Community Food Resource Center. 'For You' was played for the only time that year, and 'Racing In The Street' – always a personal favourite – felt like my own individual welcome to these shows.

27 June 2000: New York City, Madison Square Garden

‘Back In Your Arms’, ‘Mary Queen Of Arkansas’ and ‘Blinded By The Light’, all on the setlist, were among the highlights at the eighth show.

29 June 2000: New York City, Madison Square Garden

Rarities at the penultimate New York concert included 'Don't Look Back', 'The Promise' – replacing the setlisted 'Meeting Across The River' before 'Jungleland'; 'This Hard Land' and 'Growin' Up'.

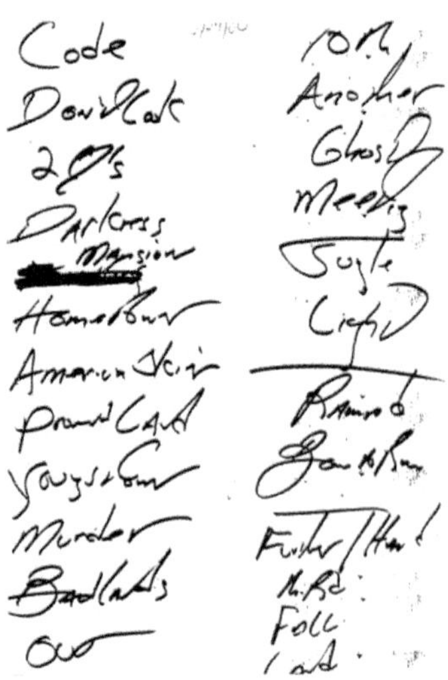

1 July 2000: New York City, Madison Square Garden

Tickets for the last night were among the toughest ever to get, being not only the finale of the 10-show Madison Square Garden run but also marking the end of the 1999-2000 Reunion tour. After no luck from any other source, I contacted Clarence Clemons' office, 15 years after I last met him, and faith was rewarded with four tickets.

Highlights included 'Lost In The Flood', first time since 1978, along with a rare 'The E Street Shuffle' and a repeat of 'The Promise'. The crowd chanted 'E Street Band' repeatedly. 'Blood Brothers' closed the tour, in a special version with an extra new last verse. For that final song, I stood arm in arm with two blood brothers, Dave and Mike, as the song says, feeling 'so many friends around me'.

During days off in the city, as Mike summarised, *'we went to a taping of the Conan O'Brien show at NBC Studios so we could see the Max Weinberg Seven in action, caught a free set by Shawn Colvin in Battery Park and went along to Little Steven's personal appearance at Tower Records.'*

Blood brothers: Mike, Dave, John, Dan and Rob, 1 July 2000, NYC

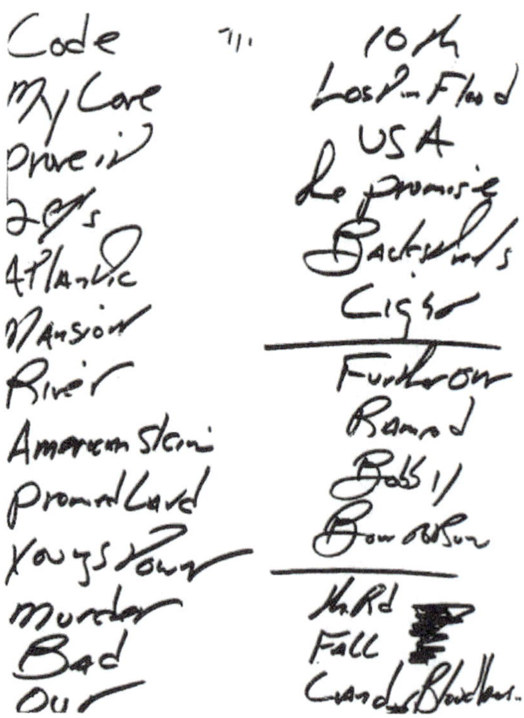

2002-2003

The *Rising* tour

14 October 2002: Paris, Palais Omnisports De Paris-Bercy

The opening night of Bruce's whistle-stop 2002 tour of Europe, and I got 'lost in the swamps of…' Paris! Staying with Mike and Dave, somehow, I managed to come out of the same hotel at a totally different side to them, causing much brief confusion and hilarity. Thanks to the season, we were glad to be indoors again on this mini-leg, before the tour moved outdoors the following year (The next show, at Barcelona, was filmed for the 'Live In Barcelona' video/DVD).

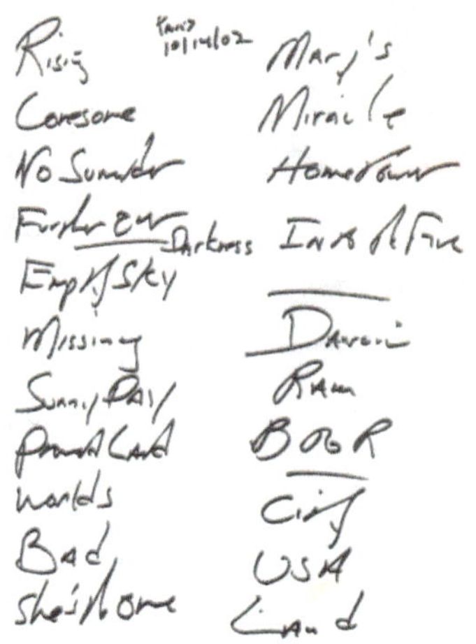

27 October 2002: London, Wembley Arena

The end of the 2002 European mini-tour, my 100th Bruce show since 1981 (thanks to Magda for champagne in the line!), and an eventful day. It was the day a major storm disrupted transport for much of the north of the UK, meaning many fans trying to head south for the concert were cut off and unable to do so. Mike, on tour up north helping Southside Johnny and the Asbury Jukes, as ticket-holder for others had to call the venue to authorise collection by a nominated friend who made it to London. He and Dave ended up at a Jukes show in Yorkshire instead, where they played 'Born To Run' in recognition of their missed Bruce event. I had a seat with my friend Chantal who had made the trip from Paris, but few others of my usual gang were present. 'Jackson Cage' was a sign request, no doubt from earlier, as it was on the set list. The 'Fooking luv ya' heckler was there again. 'Incident On 57th Street' was performed solo on the piano.

Wembley Arena 27 October 2002 - photo by SkipjackUK

6 May 2003: Rotterdam, Stadion Feyenoord

I went to the first two outdoor shows of the 2003 European leg, a chance for a mini-break with Kezia in the Rotterdam area. Bruce did a soundcheck of at least seven songs. and opened with the solo acoustic 'Born In The USA'. As at London in 2002, 'Incident On 57th Street' was solo at the piano.

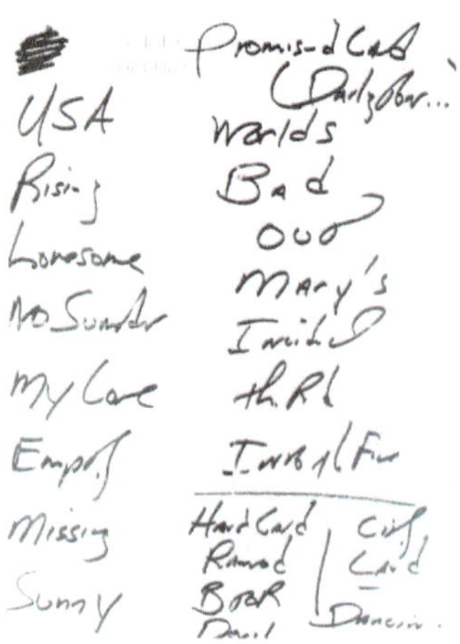

8 May 2003: Rotterdam, Stadion Feyenoord

The second Rotterdam concert started with a solo acoustic version of 'Darkness On The Edge Of Town'. 'Racing In The Street' was on the setlist, an earlier request; 'Cadillac Ranch' was an unplanned request. After one show, I met up briefly with local friend Rene before returning to Kezia at the hotel.

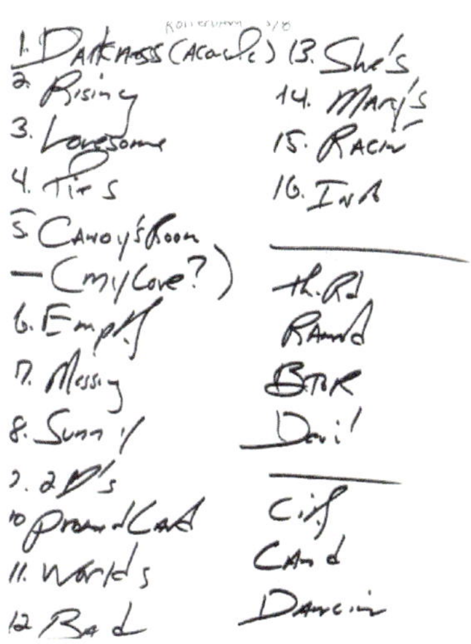

26 May 2003: London, Crystal Palace, National Sports Stadium

Meeting south of the river: an unusual new venue for Bruce in south London, and a bank holiday show in 2003. 'Meeting Across The River' (soundchecked) was a tour premiere, followed perfectly by 'Jungleland'. 'Ramrod' became an epic on this leg, with Bruce and Stevie introducing their 'Bosstime' shtick, and an extended second half involving Roy playing on his own while the whole band left the stage for a couple of minutes. 'Seven Nights To Rock' appeared for the first time in the UK, and Jon Landau guested on guitar for the finale 'Dancing In The Dark'.

27 May 2003: London, Crystal Palace, National Sports Stadium

'We're gonna play some different things for you tonight,' said Bruce, recognising many fans had also been at the first show, and proceeded to play nine different songs in the set. Treats included 'Sherry Darling', 'Racing In The Street' and unusually, a pairing of both 'Detroit Medley' and 'Seven Nights To Rock'. Jon Landau played guitar again during 'Dancing In The Dark'.

29 May 2003: Manchester, Old Trafford Cricket Ground

Another unusual UK venue for Bruce on this tour. Introducing 'Empty Sky', Bruce acknowledged that he knew 'a little bit about cricket', comparing it to baseball: 'The ball's very, very hard and you don't wanna get hit in the nuts with it…' Surprises included the UK debut of 'Loose Ends', and the first airing here of '4th Of July, Asbury Park (Sandy)' since Hammersmith in 1975 – both premieres for me.

31 May 2003: Dublin, RDS Showjumping Enclosure (Main Arena)

'I know it's late but we can make it if we run': A birthday show for me, and many friends convened for a weekend show in Dublin – Jim was last to arrive, literally running to join us. Bruce's kids were side stage, and he and Patti interacted with them now and then. 'Meeting Across The River' into 'Jungleland' was always welcome. During 'Mary's Place', Clarence was introduced as 'Emperor of all Ireland'. Joint looks of delight when we realised that we were getting 'Kitty's Back' for the first time in the UK since Hammersmith in 1975, and a live debut for most of us. It was a request played for Roberto, an Italian fan near the front who held up a sign with 'Kitty', and despite Bruce admitting the band hadn't played it for a while and might mess it up (and had no horns), it was sublime. While hamming it up with Stevie in 'Ramrod', someone gave Roy a Guinness hat, and Bruce said he had to get some fish and chips before the shop closed – and then wanted to go back to the hotel for 'one of them big, black beers that make you feel like you weigh 500 pounds!' The last time our crew saw Danny in Europe.

21 June 2003: Gothenburg, Ullevi

'Midsommar' in Sweden, and the first of many visits to a favourite venue and town, Ullevi and Gothenburg, in a country that really embraces E Street, the newspapers being filled with features, and the music playing in many bars and restaurants around show days. Clarence came out with a traditional Scandinavian wreath of flowers in his hair. Birthday boy Nils had 'Happy Birthday' sung to him in both English and Swedish. During the show, a paraglider flew over the stadium, enjoying a unique view. Bruce urged the crowd to 'get your Swedish asses out of your Swedish seats!' adding 'we gotta break the stadium again', remembering the 1985 show when they damaged the foundations. It was Roy's turn for a wreath on his head during 'Ramrod', before Bruce called 'one more for 1985!' and the tour debut of 'Twist And Shout' threatened to be a stadium breaker yet again.

Ullevi stadium with Linda – and a mural at Hotel Lorensberg

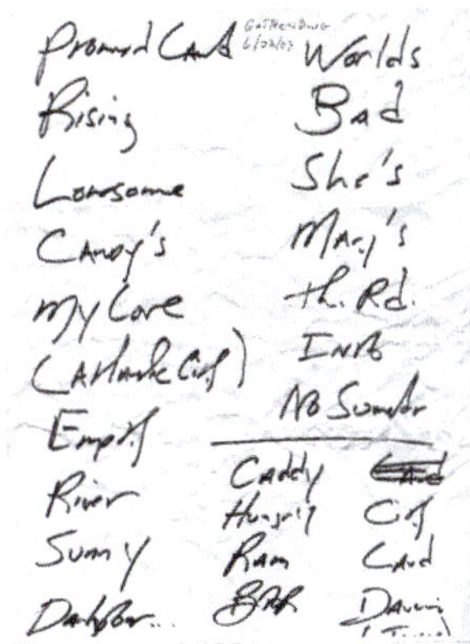

22 June 2003: Gothenburg, Ullevi

Second show ticket thanks to Helen - back in the days before there was any pit, just 'Planen' - the floor! Mike and I made our way to the far end of the front rail, and being offered 'snus' and some sort of homebrew by some young local fans...but the show itself was potent enough for us. 'Growin' Up' was a first for Sweden, dedicated to 'all the old fans out there', and 'Detroit Medley' was an extra rarity. Bruce encouraged seated fans to 'come on up for the Swedish ass-rising', and Clarence was introduced as 'honorary Swedish citizen' (he once married a Swede). Before 'My City Of Ruins' Bruce told the crowd that Sweden felt like 'a real home away from home' for them. Reminded by Stevie during 'Ramrod', 'we still got some stadium wrecking to do' - the band attempted that again with 'Twist And Shout' in 1985 tradition, this time coming back for a reprise after its first finish, due to audience chanting.

Low bridge, everybody down! On a 'Paddan' harbour boat trip

2005

The *Devils & Dust* tour

27 May 2005: London, Royal Albert Hall

The second and third shows of the solo acoustic European 'Devils & Dust' tour in 2005 saw Bruce returning to London's Royal Albert Hall. The format gave him the chance to do lesser-played songs in unusual arrangements, such as 'My Beautiful Reward' on pump organ, and 'Reason To Believe' sung with a bullet mic. 'The Wish' was a rarity (with a reference to the Queen Mother), and 'Maria's Bed', 'Cautious Man' and 'Paradise' were European debuts. 'Dream Baby Dream', Bruce's hypnotic version of the Suicide song, was the regular show closer. As on the 'Ghost Of Tom Joad' tour, Bruce took the opportunity to include some lengthy spoken introductions, and linked the two tours with the explanation that 'Matamoros Banks' was written as a sequel to 'Across The Border'. For 'The Promised Land', he recognised it was 30 years since his first visit to London.

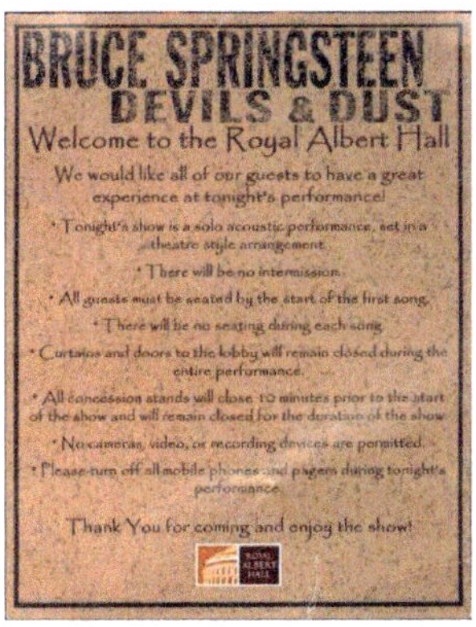

28 May 2005: London, Royal Albert Hall

'My Father's House' was soundchecked but not played; 'Black Cowboys' and 'All The Way Home' were debuts for Europe. Seven different songs from the first night, including 'Empty Sky', and piano versions of 'Two Faces', 'Real World' and 'Racing In The Street'. The 'Fookin' Luv Ya' guy heckled.

The 'walk-in' music played at venues on the 2005 tour

2006

The *Seeger Sessions* tour

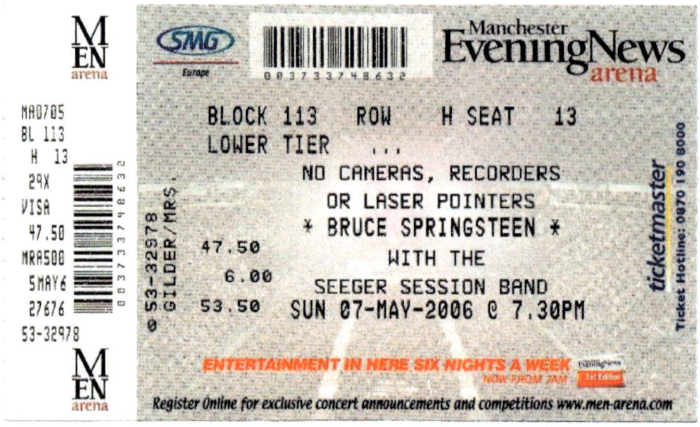

7 May 2006: Manchester, Manchester Evening News Arena

Manchester was the second show on the 2006 European tour and only the third fully public appearance by the new Seeger Sessions Band, apart from a few public rehearsals in New Jersey. Some seats were changed inside the arena at the last minute, giving some fans a different view than expected.

Even this early on, Bruce was soon changing things up, and introduced the tour debut of a unique medley/mash-up of 'Cadillac Ranch' and 'Mystery Train'. Trying to overcome challenging acoustics and some British reserve after encouraging the audience to sing, Bruce laughed: 'That's miserable!' adding 'We need some professionals!' and cued the backing singers to take over. 'John Henry' featured an extra verse about the character's burial, added at the previous show in Dublin.

Familiar as a bonus track on the 'We Shall Overcome: The Seeger Sessions' album, a cover of 'How Can I Keep From Singing' with Patti taking lead vocals was a live premiere, with only two further performances, both later that week in London.

8 May 2006: London, Hammersmith Odeon (Apollo)

Finally, Bruce was ready to return to the legendary Hammersmith Odeon, as it will always be known among fans of a certain vintage, despite later rebranding as 'Apollo'. The site of his triumphant first UK shows in 1975, Bruce was clearly highly aware of the significance of this revisit, with multiple references to the building, from his first words including 'This place looks familiar'; 'We're gonna raise the roof on this old place'; and a lengthy preamble before 'When The Saints Go Marching In':

"Oh, man, well…let me see…at this rate I'll be back in this building when I'm 88 - that ain't too old - it's getting younger every day, right? … fun to be back here, fun to be back in this place, damn … this place is one of those, uh, just, oh man, it holds a lot of ghosts for me and uh…it's just, uh, it's just been fun being, being in here tonight, really, came in that back alley - a lot of fun - but man - I thought they - I thought they like tore it down or something, I didn't even think it was still here…you know, I guess they changed the name, I guess for legal reasons, I'm not sure why - but uh, damn, this is one of those places that, uh, that I'm permanently in and it's permanently in me - so uh, I wanna thank you, London, you know - finally ready for hundreds of years old songs (chuckles) (crowd cheers)

Thanks to Brucebase for the transcription.

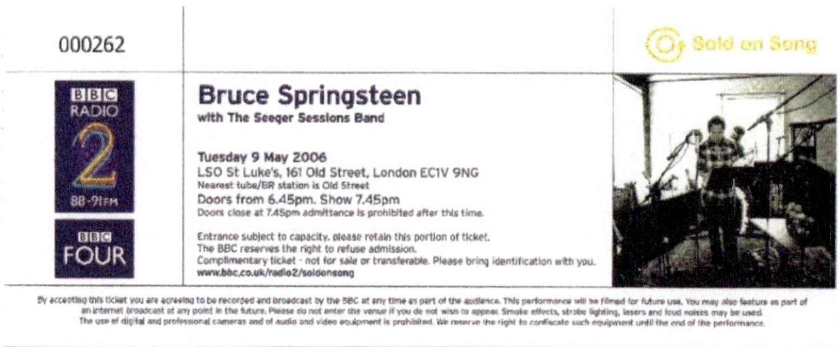

9 May 2006: London, LSO St Luke's

The filmed concert at this intimate venue for BBC TV's 'Sold On Song', originally an 18-century church, seemed an impossible ticket (maybe only 300 tickets), only available to BBC contest winners and celebs (like Emmylou Harris, Chris Evans and Harvey Goldsmith). I stood outside with my similarly ticket-less friend Carolyn, who was cursing - barely under her breath - at the lucky ticket-holders passing us to go in, and tried to keep her calm. At what seemed the last minute, someone came out with a handful of tickets and passed them out to those of us waiting. I remember the applause from our friends as we finally walked in!

DJ Johnnie Walker introduced the night, telling us we were the luckiest people anywhere - didn't we know it! Thanks to enthusiastic folks (including a few friends) in the balcony who were dubbed 'the light-shakers', Bruce repeated two songs ('Mrs McGrath' and 'O Mary Don't You Weep') for the cameras - bonus! A hilarious false solo start to 'Jacob's Ladder' before Bruce quipped: 'This is not how this song begins... it doesn't begin remotely like this! I was enjoying myself so tremendously...'

A superb culmination to three shows in three days by Bruce, and there was to be another European leg later in the year.

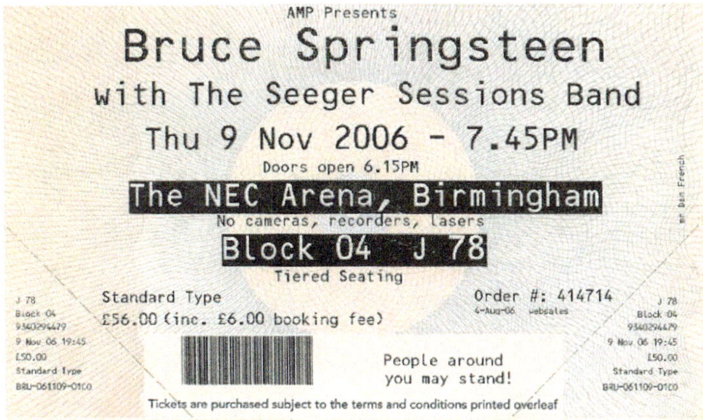

9 November 2006: Birmingham, NEC Arena

Exactly six months later, I rejoined the return leg of the 2006 European tour, for me starting at Birmingham with Bruce's fourth appearance at the NEC Arena since his first in 1981. It was immediately apparent that the setlist had evolved, opening with what was effectively a 'ska' arrangement of 'Blinded By The Light'. Nils Lofgren, who happened to be on his own UK tour, guested on 'Pay Me My Money Down', and after the other musicians had left for an encore break, he continued playing acoustic guitar. The vocal and welcoming audience brought Bruce back for an unplanned extra final encore, 'Froggie Went A-Courtin'.

11 November 2006: London, Wembley Arena

As I recall, these shows were among the first where we experienced the idea of the pit for Bruce in the UK, not just free-for-all general admission; it certainly continued from 2008 if not before. Introducing 'Growin' Up', he compared the London venue to Hammersmith six months previously, joking that everyone this night was also there, and echoing the sentiments of many about the name change: 'They'd changed it to Hammersmith Apollo, why'd they do that? I don't understand it'.

Having guested with Lucinda Williams the previous night and admiring her for being 'brave' in playing many new songs, and lamenting how US democracy was broken and needed to be fixed, Bruce introduced a 'work in progress… "Gonna Be A Long Walk Home".' The first night was the world live premiere and only tour appearance of the new song, with different lyrics unique to this performance: 'Now the water's rising 'round the corner, there's a fire burning out of control / There's a hurricane on Main Street and I've got murder in my soul.'

The show was released as part of the Nugs live archive series.

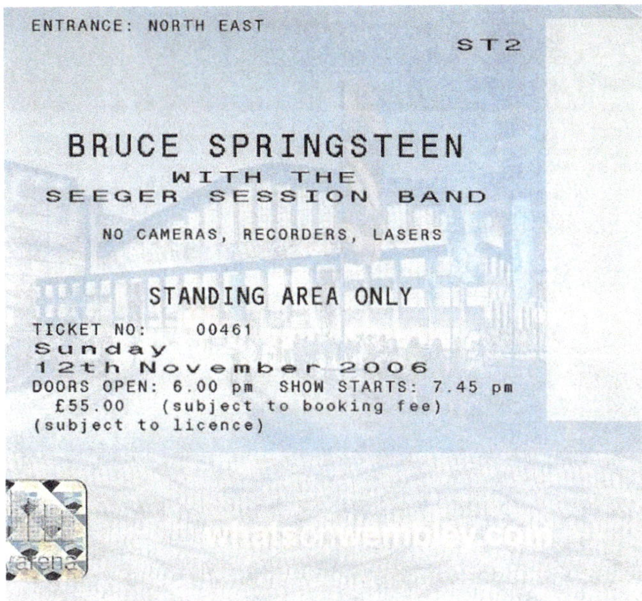

12 November 2006: London, Wembley Arena

For the second night at London, Bruce introduced the tour premiere of 'Does This Bus Stop At 82nd Street?' with 'another one from "Greetings"...' – and 'Daring Young Man On The Flying Trapeze' made its tour debut and also final appearance of three performances. In 'Long Time Comin'', Bruce talked jokingly about his young family and how he was relying on Patti to try and control them:

'I'm gonna send this one out to Patti....my lovely lady, she sends her love....I was explaining to the folks last night that we have three teenagers and, uh....those bastards simply can't be trusted....that's in the nutshell right there....no, I'm sorry, they, we did our best but they can't, that's all, we fucked it up....that's all there is to it so somebody's gotta keep an eye on 'em....she sends her love and I get to do the lazy man's work out here....'

Thanks to Brucebase for the transcription.

14 November 2006: Sheffield, Hallam FM Arena

Returning to the renamed Sheffield Arena where he'd played twice in April 1993, Bruce's final UK show in 2006 started later than expected for some unknown reason. A highlight was the tour debut of 'Youngstown', recognising Sheffield's industrial heritage, which Bruce did as a duet with Frank Bruno on guitar: 'I guess they don't make that much steel here anymore. Then again, they don't make much in Youngstown anymore, either.' 'Pay Me My Money Down' was prefaced with: 'Time to get your Sheffield arses off your Sheffield seats. This is your arse; this is your seat; separate 'em!' Making its first appearance in the UK was 'Bring 'Em Home', and 'Froggie Went A-Courtin' closed again, its last performance.

The tour continued in Ireland, finishing in Belfast after three back-to-back nights in Dublin, which were all filmed and made up the 'Live In Dublin' release…

17 November 2006: Dublin, The Point Theatre

Thanks to Damian McEvoy for this ticket! A group of us descended on Dublin for all three of Bruce's Sessions Band shows at The Point. He mentioned this band were returning to the city and venue where they'd started the 2006 European tour, describing it as 'a learning experience and a real treat'. 'Pay Me My Money Down' had an extended tuba solo by Art Baron after the other band members left the stage, with Bruce pretending to fall asleep.

As Brucebase summarises:

'"Atlantic City", "Further On (Up The Road)", "O Mary Don't You Weep", "Mrs. McGrath", "Long Time Comin'", "Pay Me My Money Down" and "Growin' Up" from this show are officially released on the Live In Dublin DVD/CD. In addition, "My City Of Ruins" is officially released on the Bruce Springsteen With The Sessions Band PBS Exclusive - a U.S. only promotional five track CD EP given to donors supporting the Public Broadcasting Service (PBS) programming with a minimum pledge of $90.'

18 November 2006: Dublin, The Point Theatre

Thank you to Linda for my ticket! 'Shenandoah' had its live premiere, and the tour (and Irish) debut of 'Highway Patrolman'. As Brucebase notes on the live releases:

'"Eyes On The Prize", "Jesse James", "My Oklahoma Home", "Highway Patrolman", "How Can A Poor Man Stand Such Times And Live?", "Jacob's Ladder", "Open All Night" and "American Land" from this show are officially released on the Live In Dublin DVD/CD. In addition, "Bobby Jean" and "Johnny 99" are officially released on the Bruce Springsteen With The Sessions Band PBS Exclusive.'

Mike, Dan, Dave and Jim at a meal in Dublin in 2006

19 November 2006: Dublin, The Point Theatre

'For You' and 'Mansion On The Hill' were soundchecked; the latter was kept until the final tour night at Belfast, but Dublin was treated to 'For You' as a tour premiere and Irish debut.

'"Old Dan Tucker", "Erie Canal", "If I Should Fall Behind", "When The Saints Go Marching In", "Blinded By The Light", "This Little Light Of Mine" and "We Shall Overcome" from this show are officially released on the Live In Dublin DVD/CD. In addition, "For You" and "The Ghost Of Tom Joad" are officially released on the Bruce Springsteen With The Sessions Band PBS Exclusive.'

Thanks to Brucebase again for the release notes.

2007-2008

The *Magic* tour

15 December 2007: Belfast, Odyssey Arena

The initial European leg of the Magic tour in 2007 was a 'whistlestop' schedule before another leg in 2008. In the UK, our first chance to catch the tour was the E Street debut at Belfast – freezing conditions, but a warm welcome from local friends. 'I'll Work For Your Love' was dedicated to Bruce's brother-in-law in attendance, and a couple who had come from their wedding to be there. Finally, 'Santa Claus Is Comin' To Town' got an airing in Britain! Ticket thanks to Magda.

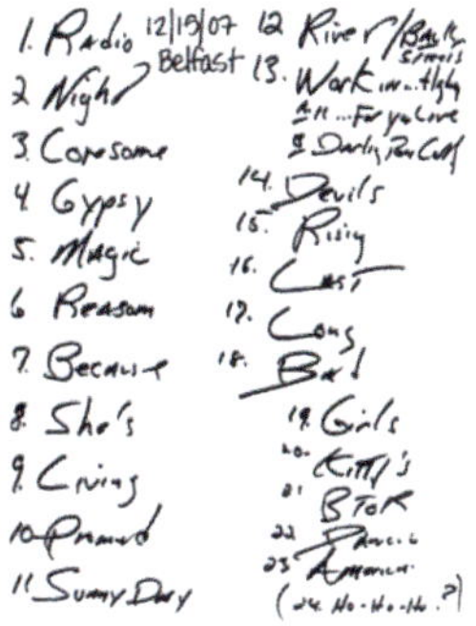

With friends at the Odyssey Arena for the Belfast show, 2007

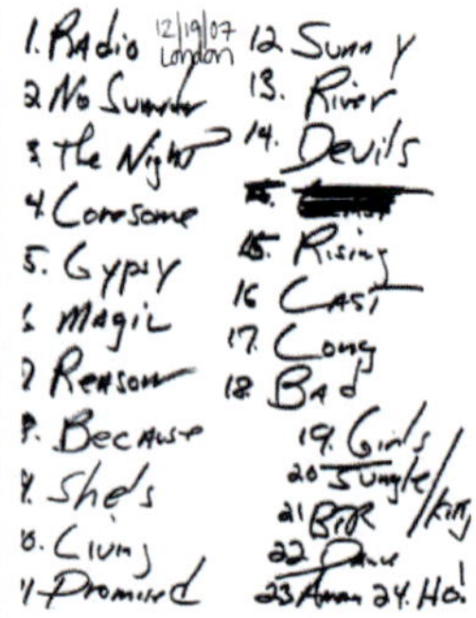

19 December 2007: London, The O2 Arena

This was a strange experience for me, since normally at a London show I would have been with many friends, but a combination of late entry (very slow organisation at the venue) and needing to leave just before the concert ended (to deal with a domestic crisis) meant that I missed meeting folks both before and after the show – I knew they were in the building around me, just not in sight.

Bruce introduced 'Magic' referring to the band as 'the big building killers', and recognising a request sign holder having followed the tour resulted in a very rare live combination of both 'Racing In The Street' and 'Jungleland' in the same set; the latter was already setlisted, but acknowledged another request from the crowd. 'Born To Run' was dedicated to 'Mike and Charlie Smith'.

'Santa Claus Is Comin' To Town' made its second UK appearance, as at Belfast complete with Santa hats on stage – Stevie ended up with a comical set of ear muffs and Santa bobble. Bruce finished the night and the 2007 tour with the promise: 'We'll see you in the summertime'.

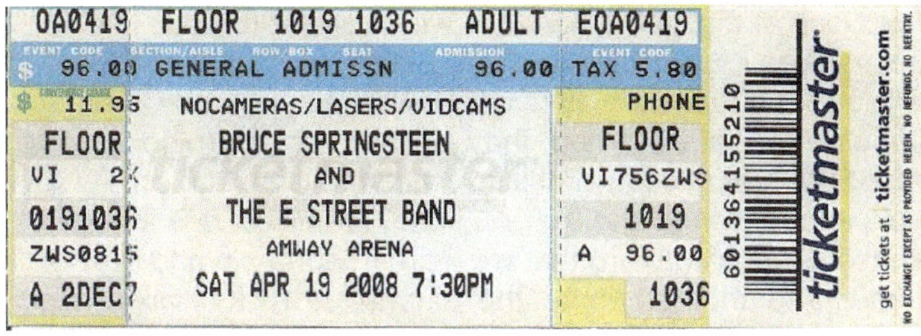

23 April 2008: Orlando, Amway Arena

On 23 April 2008, Bruce and the E Street Band rescheduled the 19 April Orlando stop on their 'Magic' tour due to the death of Danny Federici; only the second show since his funeral on the 21st, after Tampa (also rescheduled to the 22nd). By a bizarre coincidence, I just happened to be on holiday in Orlando with my wife at the time of the new show - and knew a UK friend who had a ticket for the original date, but couldn't make the new one (thank you, Keith). And so, unexpectedly, I found myself in a position to join what turned out to be the most extraordinary, emotional and cathartic experience I've had at a Springsteen show. As a fan, I hadn't lived through the loss of any band member then; this was a turning point in our relationship with E Street.

Nothing prepared me for the show's unique opening. On a darkened stage, the band filed on quietly, and - most unusually - from my position near the front, I could see they all turned their backs to the audience. Moments later, I realised why the band had made this inspired gesture to show how they joined us, the fans, in a stunning moment of respect and love which instantly dispensed with the idea of any barrier between band and crowd... a big screen started playing a video tribute to Danny: a montage of clips and photos, while the recorded 'Blood Brothers' provided a subtle soundtrack. As if this wasn't a powerful enough statement of our unity in collectively watching this homage to a mutual friend, I shall never forget when Bruce and the band turned round to face us again, and as the stage lights came on, you could see nothing but grief etched into every drawn face on stage. Goodness knows what it would have been like if they could have seen all our overwhelmed faces too. I genuinely thought to myself at that point: how can we - all - get through this? It seemed an impossible situation. But miraculously, the E Street Band found a way to deal with the apparently impossible. They did what they always manage to do, in recognition of a fellow musician; the show must go on. A couple of seconds into the first song, I realised with a huge sense of shock (again) that we were hearing a world live debut, and another tribute: the 'alternative' rock arrangement of 'Blood Brothers', as released on the EP of the same name.

The band played furiously, working through their grief, and five songs in, 'Spirit In The Night' was dedicated to Danny. This was the point at which I marvelled at the transformative power of music. What had started feeling like a funeral had somehow, within about half an hour, turned into a celebratory wake. The tear-stained faces were still there, of course, but also the sense - music being the proof - that life goes on, and we were bringing Danny with us in that realisation. 'Does This Bus Stop...', a tour debut (played in response to a request for 'Growin' Up' which Bruce explained had been played at the previous show), had rarely sounded so joyous. 'Fire' was the result of a 'pick the song' vote on a local radio station, with references from Bruce to Elvis and covers by Robert Gordon and Babyface Edmonds.

The last thing I was expecting towards the end of this show was a guest appearance, but Roger McGuinn took the stage, and like so often that night, the song choice seemed poignantly perfect as the jangling guitars rang out: 'Turn! Turn! Turn! (To Everything There Is A Season)'. We were treated to a second Byrds classic: 'Mr Tambourine Man'. (Fittingly, video and audio of 'Turn! Turn! Turn! (To Everything There Is A Season)' was officially released on the 'Magic Tour Highlights' download EP that summer, with proceeds supporting the Danny Federici Melanoma Fund).

A unique, landmark event of unity, simultaneously heartbreaking and later joyous; and what a privilege to be there by chance... From one DPF to another: RIP, Phantom Dan. Thank you for all those years since I first saw you in concert; your bandmates did you proud, and then some.

4/23/08
Orlando, FL

1. Blood
2. Night
3. Radio
4. Lonesome [?]
5. Spirit...
6. River
7. Candy
8. prove it
9. She's
10. Livin
11. Promised [?]
12. Fire
13. Lost
14. Devils
15. Rising
16. Last
17. Long [?]
18. Bad
19. Turn
20. Tambourine
21. Kitty's Back
22. BTBR [?]
23. Glory
24. American

22 May 2008: Dublin, RDS Arena

The 2008 European leg started with three Dublin shows in four days at the RDS Arena. Curiously, none of the tickets mentioned the venue itself. A front pit on the pitch was a standard feature at stadiums now, although specified 'pit tickets' had yet to become a familiar option. We missed the pit allocation that first day, but allowed more time getting in after that, and later regularly secured pit spaces when standing. Southside Johnny guested on 'Tenth Avenue Freeze-Out'. This was the day our gang unveiled the original private edition 'E Street Kings / We are the…' t-shirts, adapting Bruce's onstage 'legendary E Street Band' introduction.

The first 'It'd Be Rude Not To' Crew t-shirts, May 2008

23 May 2008: Dublin, RDS Arena

This leg of the tour also saw the first use of new extra vertical screens either side of the stage, continuing ever since, and the beginning of the 'E!' 'STREET!' 'BAND!' graphics on the screens during the band introductions. Bruce teased the crowd that they couldn't all have been present the previous night, but promised to 'switch it all up for you tonight' anyway, and played 'Night', 'No Surrender' and 'Girls In Their Summer Clothes' as alternatives and live debuts for Ireland. After the latter, Bruce was given a beer by someone in the audience and drank it, toasting 'To the Irish girls… I owe somebody a beer now!' During the 'Boss-time' routine in 'Glory Days', he wondered if it was 'Guinness time?'

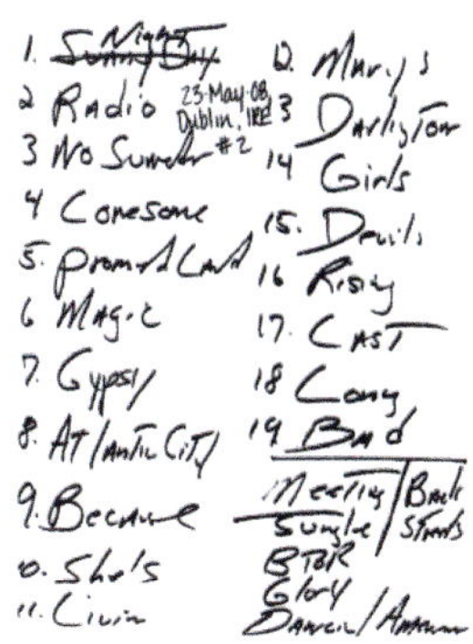

25 May 2008: Dublin, RDS Arena

'The last dance in Dublin' brought more setlist changes by Bruce, with the first Irish performances of 'The Ties That Bind', 'Spirit In The Night' (getting up close and personal with fans at the front), and '4th Of July, Asbury Park (Sandy)'. The last was dedicated to recently deceased Danny, with thanks for all the condolences received for him. Bruce reminisced about Danny's troublemaking before 'Growin' Up', recalling when he 'parked his car in a tow-away zone with a huge marijuana plant on the front seat'... having decided to go to the police station and explain his car was stolen, despite Bruce's warning, Danny abruptly got arrested on arrival. Bruce summed up: 'I'm sure he had to be Irish!'

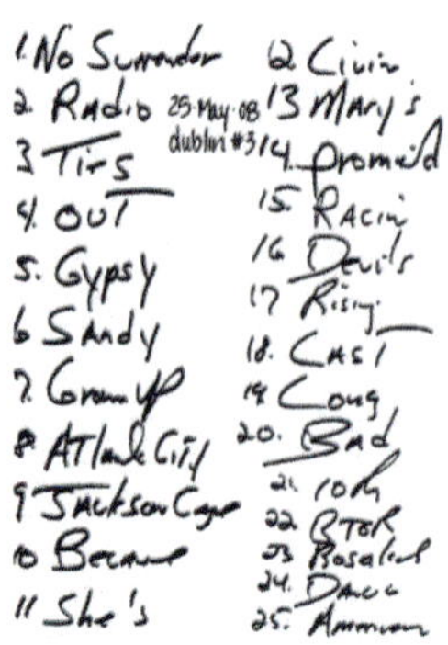

28 May 2008: Manchester, Old Trafford

The Manchester stage was moved forward, obstructing the view for some seats, and there were problems with the sound to begin with. 'Magic' was introduced with a reference to Bruce's eldest son Evan being a 'soccer' fan – 'these are his boys right here in England.' Bruce having encouraged request signs to be passed up, 'It's Hard To Be A Saint In The City' and 'Darlington County' were requests, and 'I'll Work For Your Love' was a UK live debut, replacing the setlisted 'Waitin' On A Sunny Day' / 'Lost In The Flood' options. 'Growin' Up' was dedicated to Brad, a kid with 'big freaky red headsets'. The date also marked Mike's 100th Bruce show, as confirmed with an unofficial certificate!

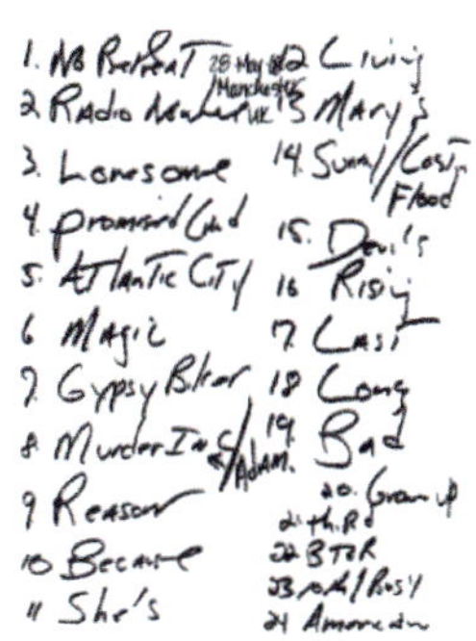

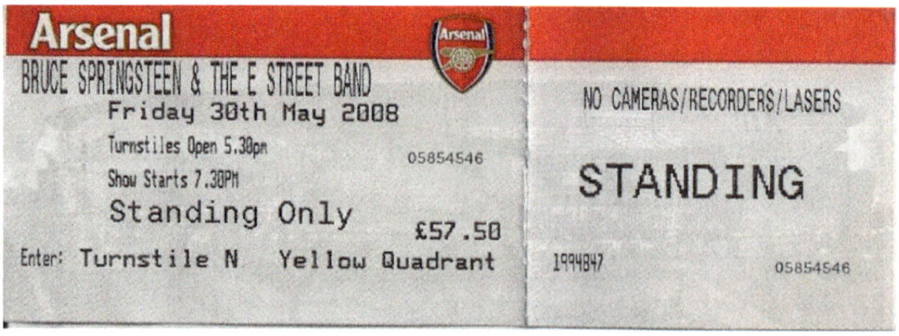

30 May 2008: London, Emirates Stadium

Bruce and the band came to 'baptise' the Emirates Stadium 'with a little bit of rock and roll'. He joked that if 'nobody's played here… we gotta test that structure tonight.' For some time just the 30 May show was announced, but I kept my fingers crossed they'd add another on the following day – my birthday – and sure enough, they did.

'Cadillac Ranch' and 'Point Blank' were played as requests, the latter unfortunately causing many to take a break or just chatter during the song.

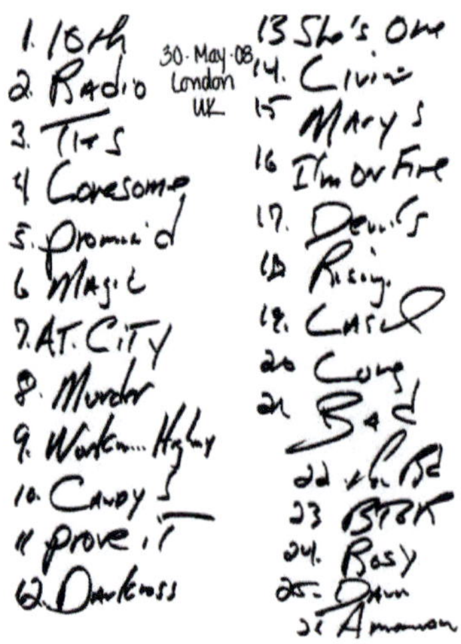

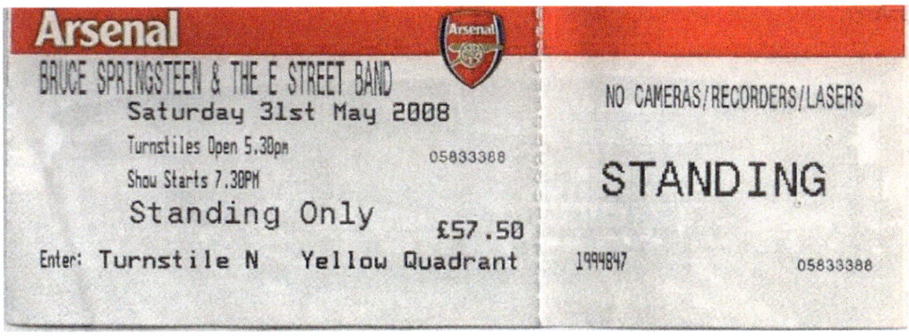

31 May 2008: London, Emirates Stadium

My 50th birthday, complete with pre-show cake and candles, and Bruce played a venue within an hour of my hometown. Before '4th Of July, Asbury Park (Sandy)', Bruce encouraged and collected request signs, musing aloud about their value. He retold the story about Danny and the marijuana plant, adding that he was a kleptomaniac who stole jukebox speakers and elevator lights. Two tour premieres featured: 'Downbound Train' was played in response to a request sign reading 'No Job No Girl – Downbound Train' ('This man obviously has no job and no pride'), and 'I'm On Fire' ('Here's one we ain't played') saw Bruce sitting on a chair at the front edge of the stage. 'Backstreets' was a request, with Bruce opening a small piece of paper. There's been divided opinion as to whether he dedicated it to 'Dad' (Philip Jump's daughter Molly submitted a request) or 'Dan' (due to secret plans by my friends). Either way – thanks for the thought, folks!

'The smallest request out there…'

My 50th birthday 'pass' by Dave

The 'It'd Be Rude Not To' crew help me celebrate my 50th birthday

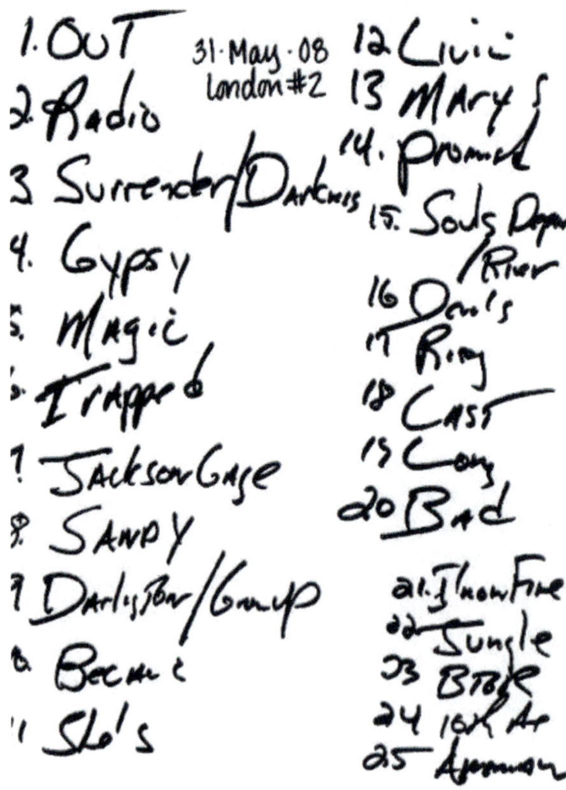

31·May·08
London #2

1. OUT
2. Radio
3 Surrender/Darkness
4. Gypsy
5. Magic
6. Trapped
7 JacksonCage
8 Sandy
9 Darlington/GrowUp
10 Because
11 Sho's
12 Civic
13 Mary's
14. Promd
15. Souls Depd/River
16 Devil's
17 Ring
18 Cast
19 Long
20 Bad
21. I know Fire
22 Jungle
23 BTBR
24 10th Av
25 Apoman

14 June 2008: Cardiff, Millennium Stadium

Bruce and the band's first ever show in Wales, which he recognised with his introduction to the European debut of 'From Small Things (Big Things One Day Come)', noting 'This is our Welsh connection right here', a nod to local rocker Dave Edmunds, to whom Bruce had given the song in 1981. 'Blinded By The Light' was one of several sign requests, dedicated to Danny with a long story about having to play to get bail money for Danny and Vini back in the late 60s after they'd both been arrested for 'interfering' with police; 'Danny had been 'smoking a little something' again. 'Jungleland' was played 'for Tom and Hannah', and 'Thunder Road' was in memory of US journalist Tim Russert, a 'long-time friend of the E Street Band', and 'a strong voice for honesty and accountability'.

4 July 2008: Gothenburg, Ullevi

Bruce celebrated the US holiday in Sweden with several 'Fourth of July specials', opening with the full-band 'Born In The USA' and broadcasting 10 tracks on Sirius internet radio: '4th Of July, Asbury Park (Sandy)', 'Atlantic City', 'Independence Day' and others. Both Danny and Madam Marie, recently deceased, were remembered. 'Be True' had its Swedish live debut, dedicated to someone Bruce met outside his hotel, and 'This Hard Land' and 'Rosalita (Come Out Tonight)' were played as sign requests.

Thanks to Clarence's office, we had our first experience of the E Street Lounge, where Little Steven was holding court and greeting everyone. I introduced my friends to him, adding in Mike's case that he worked for Southside Johnny. 'Southside?' said Stevie, 'That guy never listens to a word I say!' He and Mike are pictured sharing the joke…

5 July 2008: Gothenburg, Ullevi

Bruce rewarded Swedish devotion the second night with 17 different songs out of the 28 played; having soundchecked 'Drive All Night' both days, it had its first airing since 1981. 'Summertime Blues', 'Backstreets' (unusually early in the set, as Bruce commented), 'Roulette' and 'Janey, Don't You Lose Heart' were among the other rarities, most played by sign request, as was 'Twist And Shout' – by now the traditional 'stadium breaker'. 'The authorities have told us not to play this song… we have been told we cannot play this song… this is the stadium breaker right here…'

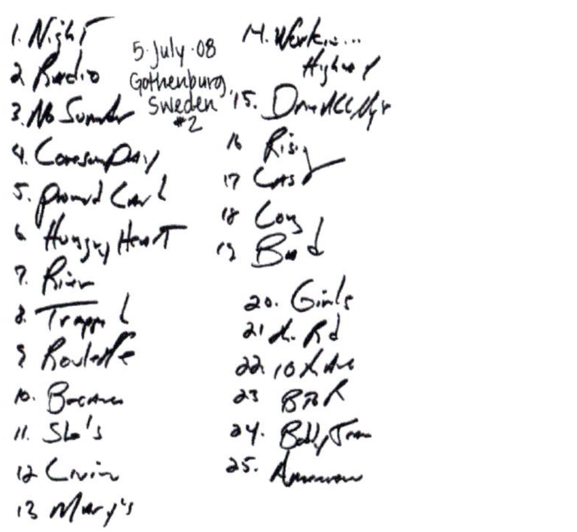

19 July 2008: Barcelona, Camp Nou

After several concerts in May, June and July, we wrapped up our own 'Magic' tour plans with the two final European shows in 2008, at Barcelona. We stayed at the same hotel we'd used in 1999, Flor Parks in La Rambla. Given the Spanish summer heat, some of us decided to have seats for the first night, and some would stand for the second show. With thanks to our ticket angel Holly, now working for Soozie Tyrell, a couple more E Street lounge passes were secured for both nights.

'Janey, Don't You Lose Heart' (its Spanish live debut), 'Waitin' On A Sunny Day' and 'Backstreets' were all played by sign request, and 'Summertime Blues' and 'Twist And Shout' had return performances.

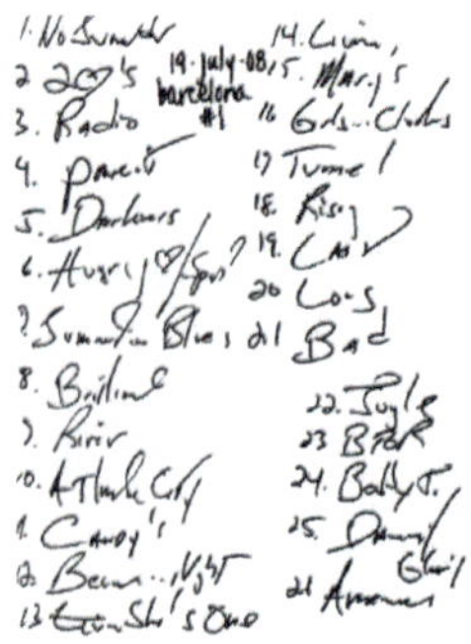

20 July 2008: Barcelona, Camp Nou

After a 34-year wait, I completed my live set of all the 'Born In The USA' songs with the rarely-played 'I'm Goin' Down', its European premiere thanks to an ingenious scrolling electronic request sign which Bruce brought on stage and enjoyed displaying. During the encore 'American Land', Springsteen family members and friends were on stage, with Bruce's son Evan given a namecheck.

Standing at the front left corner of the pitch before the show with Helen, we got chatting to a tall guy there on his own – the start of a special friendship since with Winni, a German living in Zaragoza.

As if the concert itself wasn't memorable enough, three of us had an eventful return to the city centre, especially Mike, as he vividly recalled:

'After the show, with Sunday night public transport shutting down, Dan, Dave and I chose to take a slow three-mile walk through the backstreets of Barcelona to our hotel. As we got to La Rambla, we were quickly surrounded by a gang of young women. Our first instinct was to assume they were on their way home after a girls' night out and were feeling no pain and probably a bit frisky. As if to illustrate that thought, one of them then grabbed me by the nuts and showed no sign of releasing her vice-like grip. A very small part of my brain may

have extremely briefly entertained the idea that my luck was in, but my thoughts soon turned to finding a means of escape. Dan and Dave had already done just that, hiding in the doorway of a nearby bar that was closing for the night. Eventually I was set free, the women ran off laughing and we made it back to the hotel in one piece. It was only when I emptied my pockets before going to bed that I noticed they were less full than they had been when we left the stadium. To be more specific, 50 Euros and my Bruce ticket were no longer there. It was then that we realised the girls had been professional thieves (La Rambla is full of them) and their loud behaviour had been a distraction technique. While one performed the Nutcracker Suite, her accomplice dipped into my pocket and helped herself to my cash. I didn't feel a thing. Luckily, she didn't take my phone too, which was also in that pocket. Thankfully I'd already used the Bruce ticket. You live and learn. It's a funny story now.'

Thanks to Soozie – via Holly – Dave joined Harry & Gill with E Street Lounge passes for the Barcelona shows, 2008

2009

The *Working On A Dream* tour

4 June 2009: Stockholm, Stockholms Stadion

Having been to Gothenburg on Sweden's west coast for shows previously, it was the turn of Stockholm on the east coast in 2009. Although it was June, that early in the season meant unpredictable Baltic conditions, and our abiding memories of those days was cold, breezy and sometimes damp weather – not ideal for three outdoor stadium shows, but when in Sweden…

Nils Lofgren reflected on his Swedish ancestry by opening each of the three Stockholm shows with an instrumental accordion version of 'Idas Sommarvisa', a song linked to local Astrid Lindgren, while the band took to the stage; its summer theme was then balanced by the full band version of 'Who'll Stop The Rain'. Due to TV filming commitments, Max Weinberg was replaced at these shows (and some others in 2009) by his 18-year-old son Jay. Max's daughter Ali guested on accordion for 'American Land', and Clarence's son Jarod held up the request sign received for 'I'm Goin' Down'. 'Wild Thing' (another request), 'Kingdom Of Days' and 'The Wrestler' were rarities and highlights on this first night.

Bruce spoke a little in Swedish, referring to being 'back in my home in Sweden', recognising his long-standing and ongoing special relationship with the country since 1975. Once he fell on the stage, slippery from the steady rain, and joked 'I broke my ass… my ass is broken… ass-breaking time' during 'Glory Days', to which Stevie replied: 'You got another cheek – it's Boss-time!' 'Twist And Shout', a final request, followed in true stadium-breaking tradition.

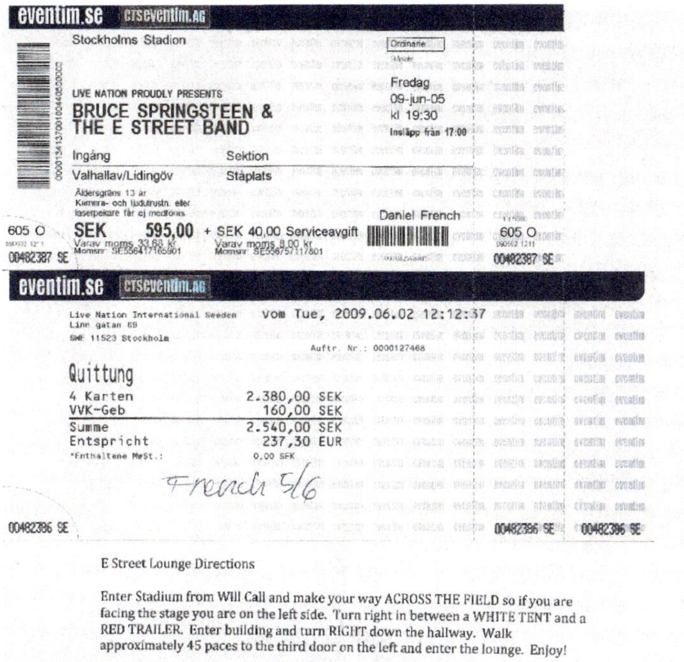

eventim.se ctseventim.AG

Stockholms Stadion

Ordinarie

LIVE NATION PROUDLY PRESENTS
BRUCE SPRINGSTEEN &
THE E STREET BAND

Fredag
09-jun-05
kl 19:30
Insläpp från 17:00

Ingång	Sektion
Valhallav/Lidingöv	Ståplats

Åldersgräns 13 år
Kamera- och ljudutrustn. eller
laserpekare får ej medföras

Daniel French

605 O

SEK 595,00 + SEK 40,00 Serviceavgift
Varav moms 33,68 kr
Momsnr SE556417165901
Varav moms 8,00 kr
Momsnr SE556757117801

00482387 SE

eventim.se ctseventim.AG

Live Nation International Sweden
Linngatan 69
SWE 11523 Stockholm

vom Tue, 2009.06.02 12:12:37

Auftr. Nr.: 0000127468

Quittung

4 Karten	2.380,00 SEK
VVK-Geb	160,00 SEK
Summe	2.540,00 SEK
Entspricht	237,30 EUR
*Enthaltene MwSt.:	0,00 SEK

French 5/6

00482386 SE

E Street Lounge Directions

Enter Stadium from Will Call and make your way ACROSS THE FIELD so if you are facing the stage you are on the left side. Turn right in between a WHITE TENT and a RED TRAILER. Enter building and turn RIGHT down the hallway. Walk approximately 45 paces to the third door on the left and enter the lounge. Enjoy!

5 June 2009: Stockholm, Stockholms Stadion

Thanks to Clarence again, I bought four tickets with E Street Lounge passes for the second show at Stockholm. We met a new friend, Paul, there, introduced by Astrid, who we'd met previously in the lounge. Also, there was an older guy seemingly on his own, looking like he felt a little out of place, so we had a chat with him, something like this:

Him: 'Hello, I'm a potato farmer. My name is Nils.'
Us: 'What a coincidence - you'll love the show tonight; there's a guy in the band also called Nils!'
Him: 'Oh yes, I know, he's my nephew.'

Uncle Nils! As soon as he said that, the family resemblance was obvious – he did look a lot like an older version of Nils. We took a photo with him, but sadly most of the image got damaged somehow – maybe the damp Swedish weather. It turned out Uncle Nils wasn't alone, but with a group of family members. At some point they got ushered through to a guest enclosure by someone calling 'Lofgrens! Lofgrens!' Uncle Nils encouraged us to walk in with him, and so we joined the group, feeling we had become honorary Lofgrens that day.

Another cold and wet evening, and one sign asked Bruce 'How is your ass?' after 'breaking' it at the previous show! He replied 'I fell down last night but it's good...' 'Good Lovin' had its live debut, often the time when Bruce would collect request signs. Requested by a seven-year-old girl using a crown-shaped sign, 'Queen Of The Supermarket' made its live debut and only appearance on the tour. The same girl was chosen to sing during 'Waitin' On A Sunny Day', and Bruce said 'Oh, you're better than yesterday...' as she'd apparently sung on the song at the previous concert. Other requests included 'Growin' Up' and 'Lost In The Flood' – the latter described by Bruce as 'very rarely played... I think we remember it...' In the 'Bosstime' routine during 'Glory Days', the cold was obviously affecting the musicians, and Bruce observed: 'Steve, I gotta go home, man, I can't feel my fingers!'

Paul's Stockholm request sign *Uncle Nils!*

7 June 2009: Stockholm, Stockholms Stadion

'Fade Away', a soundchecked request, was played for the first time with the band since 1981 (it had featured at a few solo 2005 shows), and it was its European debut. Bruce introduced it as Stevie's favourite song, saying it was the first sign he'd seen for it, adding it was a soul song all about 'some lessons in the art of appropriate begging' for forgiveness. 'The River' and 'Surprise, Surprise' were tour premieres, the latter another request, and 'Mony Mony' made its European debut. Ali Weinberg returned to guest on accordion again for 'American Land'. Before 'Thunder Road', Bruce said in Swedish: 'I want to thank my Swedish fans here in Stockholm for three fantastic nights… you are the best… we love you.'

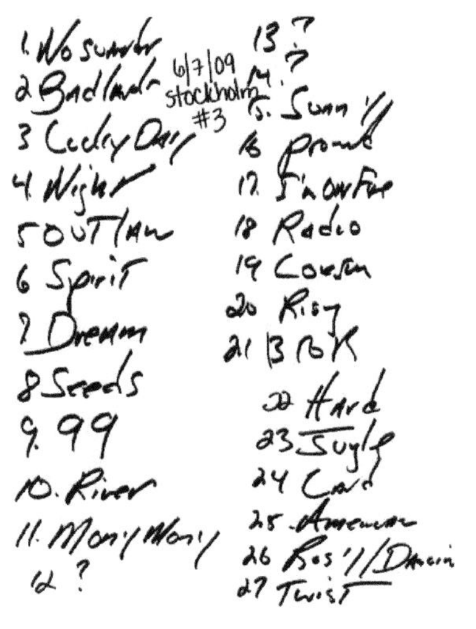

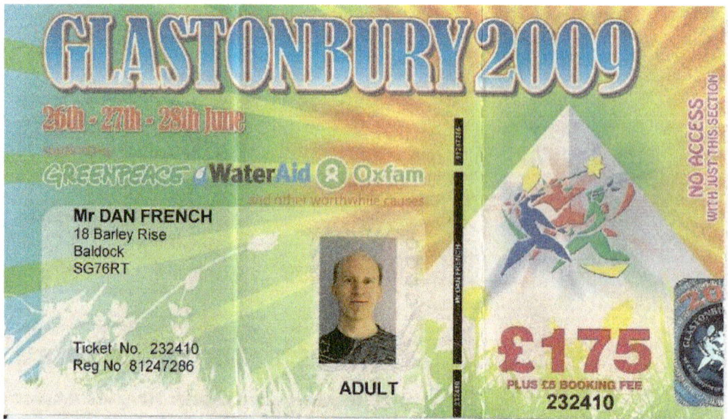

27 June 2009: Glastonbury festival

Eternal thanks to Helen for inviting me along to the Glastonbury experience! She reasoned that the crowd would move during the performers before Bruce's headline set, and sure enough with that strategy we ended up on the front rail at the left side, where he just happened to go walkabout and climbed the barrier in front of us, during 'Raise Your Hand'. People were clambering behind us to get closer, and I literally had to hang on to the backs of Bruce's legs to stay upright. Somehow, I got my camera hand free, and thought I was shooting video, but accidentally got a few extreme close-up stills instead. A unique cover of Joe Strummer's festival song 'Coma Girl' was the opener.

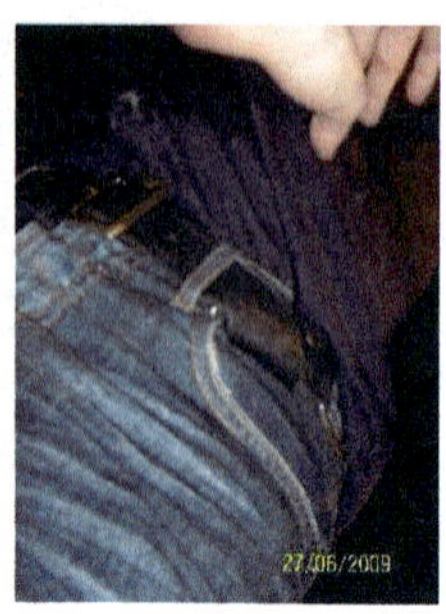

28 June 2009: London, Hard Rock Calling

Again with major thanks to Helen, we made the trip from Glastonbury to London overnight to join other friends for the Hyde Park festival. Having missed Bruce guesting with The Gaslight Anthem the previous day, we caught his repeat performance on 'The '59 Sound' here, and frontman Brian Fallon returned the favour by joining the E Street Band for 'No Surrender', as he'd done at Glastonbury. The Strummer connection continued with an appropriate 'London Calling' up first, its European debut. Bruce played several songs from sign requests, including 'Bobby Jean', 'Trapped', 'No Surrender' and 'Jungleland'.

The stage having an unusually high set of steps, Bruce joked in no uncertain words that due to his age, he needed help getting up it: 'Somebody get me a fucking elevator! I'm fucking sixty!' During the 'Glory Days' routine with Stevie, Bruce asked him as usual: 'What time is it?' Stevie's answer was: 'It's curfew-breakin' Boss-time!' Little did anyone know the local curfew, being a residential area, would haunt them next time in Hyde Park…

Having been first broadcast on TV, Bruce's headline set was officially released on DVD and Blu-Ray as 'London Calling: Live In Hyde Park'.

5 July 2009: Vienna, Ernst Happel Stadion

Nils continued his 2009 tradition of opening the show with a local-themed instrumental on accordion, this time 'An der schönen blauen Donau (The Blue Danube Waltz)'. Plenty of sign requests were played, including 'Growin' Up', 'Rendezvous', 'Proud Mary', '4th Of July, Asbury Park (Sandy)', 'Because The Night' and 'Jersey Girl'. 'Proud Mary' was a European debut. 'Into The Fire' and '4th Of July, Asbury Park (Sandy)' were 2009 tour premieres. Bruce spotted a woman with a bright 'Jersey Girl' shirt, which she took off and passed to him, prompting his amused dedication: 'Well, I never expected that, but… guess we're gonna have to do this one for you… we've never played this one out of the States…'

Vienna 2009 poster

Astrid, Vienna – photo by Mike Saunders

11 July 2009: Dublin, RDS Arena

'Fields of Athenry' was the traditional instrumental played by Nils on accordion to open both weekend nights in Dublin. The first show featured an early first onstage appearance of Jake Clemons, guesting with his uncle Clarence on saxophone for 'Tenth Avenue Freeze-Out', three years before he would become a regular additional player following the death of Clarence. Sign requests played were 'You Can Look (But You Better Not Touch)' (also a tour premiere), 'Seven Nights To Rock', 'For You', 'Thunder Road' (setlisted) and 'Because The Night'. Evan Springsteen guested on acoustic guitar during 'American Land'.

Jake Clemons made his E Street guest debut – photo from Flickr

12 July 2009: Dublin, RDS Arena

Bruce rang the changes for the second show in Dublin, including requests for 'Spirit In The Night' ('for Lucy'), 'Sherry Darling', 'Proud Mary' (both Irish debuts), 'Prove It All Night' and 'Trapped'. 'American Skin (41 Shots)' was soundchecked and performed for the first time in Europe. Having slipped on the rainy stage on the Saturday night, Bruce reacted to a safety-conscious sign: 'Caution – slippery when wet – we don't want you to break that nice ass!' Clearly very familiar with Irish culture and institutions now after many visits, Bruce made multiple local references during 'Working On A Dream'. 'Waitin' On A Sunny Day' saw a rare missed catch by tech Kevin Buell when Bruce wildly mis-threw his acoustic guitar to him: 'Sorry, Kev!' 'Glory Days' once again used the back-and-forth routine between Bruce and Stevie about the curfew, with Stevie declaring: 'It's curfew-busting Boss time!'

Some of the crew pull grumpy faces at the rain, first night in Dublin

14 July 2009: Glasgow, Hampden Park

The first E Street Band show in Glasgow and only their third Scottish concert after two in Edinburgh in 1981, so two thirds of the setlist were firsts for Scotland. Nils's opening accordion instrumental was 'Flower Of Scotland', and 'Pink Cadillac' (a request) returned after not being played since 2003. 'Cover Me' was another sign request, but the undoubted highlight was 'Incident On 57th Street', heralded with a massive sign as big as Bruce himself. Big Neil, our friend in Glasgow, celebrated his 100th Bruce show here, fittingly on home turf with family and friends, and this was one of his favourite Springsteen songs. Bruce's eldest son Evan returned to play acoustic guitar on 'American Land' again, as in Dublin.

2 August 2009: Santiago De Compostela, Auditorio Monte Do Gozo

The 2009 European tour finale, and the local opening instrumental for the Galicia region of Spain was 'A Rianxeira', played solo as usual by Nils on accordion. Three major rarities, all sign requests: 'Burning Love' (first live performance), 'Born To Be Wild' (Spanish premiere) and 'This Life' (European debut). Clarence's final European show.

A poorly organised and over-booked event, with some of the 40,000 ticket holders unable to enter the outdoor venue, which had ineffective security and safety hazards. Lack of local transport coordination meant our group and others missed shuttle buses back, and had little choice other than a long walk home to our hotel in the city. Personally, I almost didn't make the show, as that day I felt extremely unwell with abdominal pain and could only rest up, while the others went ahead to queue. When shortly before gates were due to open, I suddenly felt some relief, it seemed – appropriately for a pilgrimage site - like a miracle, and a quick taxi ride meant I caught up with the gang in time to deliver Helen's ticket and pit pass, and got through the evening on sheer adrenaline.

2012-2013

The *Wrecking Ball* tour

17 May 2012: Barcelona, Estadi Olímpic Lluís Companys

Having last seen Bruce in Spain, a bunch of us returned there to catch two Barcelona shows early in the 2012 European tour. From outside the stadium, most of the soundcheck songs could be identified, apart from an unknown (and abandoned) band workout featuring the singers in gospel style. This show is famous as one when a sign request really paid off, specifying 'With Intro 78 Prove It All Night', resulting in Bruce reviving the extended version with piano and guitar introduction, not heard live since 1980, also being a European debut, as was 'Talk To Me'. 'You Can Look (But You Better Not Touch)' had been rehearsed at soundcheck and was a tour premiere here, another being 'Hungry Heart', with an unexpected sax solo. Connor's first show.

18 May 2012: Barcelona, Estadi Olímpic Lluís Companys

A satisfying proportion of song changes at the second show in Barcelona, including an opening 'Night', 'The Ties That Bind', 'Two Hearts', 'Spirit In The Night' (a request), 'The E Street Shuffle', 'Trapped' (rehearsed the previous day), 'Downbound Train', 'Because The Night', 'Working On The Highway', 'Racing In The Street' and 'Ramrod'.

While waiting in line, a certain Sole Driver immortalised our spot with barrier graffiti…

21 June 2012: Sunderland, Stadium Of Light

Bruce's first show at Sunderland, and Nils's birthday, as Bruce mentioned in the band introductions during 'My City Of Ruins'. A cool wet day, and Bruce remarked the weather was what he expected: 'Give me some of that English rain!' The first performance of 'Spirit In The Night' in the UK since 1975; other rarities included 'Does This Bus Stop At 82nd Street?' (Bruce joking that someone in the crowd stole his microphone) and 'Point Blank'. After losing a guitar string or two while playing 'Seven Nights To Rock', Bruce shrugged: 'I don't need all them strings!' Connor and Chris had a sign asking to dance with birthday boy Nils, and both got their wish during 'Dancing In The Dark'.

Jim with a different Gill (Dove), Sunderland

22 June 2012: Manchester, Etihad stadium

A very wet day (as so often in Manchester), mostly spent sheltering in the hotel, where I met John & Tom W for the first time – our paths must have crossed at many shows before without us knowing.

Rarities included another successful sign request for 'Prove It All Night' with the '78 intro, a solo piano rendition of 'The Promise', 'Save My Love' (all debuts for the UK), 'Cadillac Ranch' and 'Twist And Shout'. Curt Ramm and his trumpet went flying while he was playing, when he slipped and fell while coming forward on the stage, causing Bruce to declare near the end: 'We can't do no more, somebody's gonna get hurt!'

John W and son Tom with the Badlands group, Manchester

24 June 2012: Isle of Wight, Seaclose Park

Bruce's Isle of Wight debut continued his taste for festival appearances, with the setlist reflecting the diverse audience. Having planned 'Prove It All Night' with the '78 intro, 'Because The Night' was a safer option. 'Save My Love' / 'The Promised Land' were dropped, and 'Born In The USA' was chosen over 'Thunder Road'. Curt Ramm was introduced: 'and his flying trumpet!' A fireworks display closed the headline set while the band played 'Twist And Shout', and wrapped up the UK dates for that month. Sky Arts TV broadcast four songs.

On the Isle of Wight ferry

Unusual headgear

4 July 2012: Paris, Palais Omnisports De Paris-Bercy

Bruce celebrated the Fourth of July in 2012 on his first of two nights at Paris with Independence Day specials: '4th Of July, Asbury Park (Sandy)', 'Darlington County' and a solo piano 'Independence Day'. The opening accordion intro was 'La Vie En Rose', associated with Edith Piaf, played by both Roy and Charlie. 'Easy Money' had its European debut due to Patti being present for the duet. Thanks to Linda for my ticket! Fittingly, both this and the following concert were officially issued by Nugs in the live archive audio series, and 'Independence Day' was an official video release.

5 July 2012: Paris, Palais Omnisports De Paris-Bercy

After the initial accordion rendition of 'Au Clair De La Lune' by Roy and Charlie, Bruce astonished everyone including the band for the second Paris show, opening with six unexpected songs before the usual 'We Take Care Of Our Own' opener, including a rare 'Something In The Night'. For the first time since 1978, both 'Incident On 57th Street' and 'Racing In The Street' featured in the same setlist. 'I'm Goin' Down' was another rarity, 'Easy Money' with Patti returned, and 'For You' made its tour debut, as a solo piano performance. The 'Apollo Medley' ('The Way You Do The Things You Do' and '634-5789 (Soulsville, USA)') was played both nights, the last times in Europe. Bruce's daughter was the 'Dancing In The Dark' girl, cheered on by his family; he dedicated 'We Are Alive' to his mother and also mentioned his sister in its introduction. As with the first night, Nugs released the official audio recording of the concert.

Family femmes in Paris: Bruce's mother-in-law Patricia, youngest sister Pam, mother Adele and daughter Jessica helped him celebrate

14 July 2012: London, Hyde Park

After watching John Fogerty play at Hard Rock Calling earlier in the lineup, Bruce joined him on 'Rockin' All Over The World', and Fogerty returned the favour for 'The Promised Land' during Bruce's headline set. Tom Morello, also earlier on the bill, guested with Bruce on 'Death To My hometown' and 'The Ghost Of Tom Joad'. Bruce opened his set playing 'Thunder Road' with just Roy on piano, saying that he remembered this opening song at Hammersmith in 1975.A sign request led to a unique tour performance of 'Take 'Em As They Come'.

Paul McCartney guested to play encores 'I Saw Her Standing There' and 'Twist And Shout', but over-keen organisers promptly cut the audio at the 10.30pm curfew. Bruce sang a part of 'Goodnight Irene' without any amplified sound, and his farewell comments were mostly inaudible. The incident is still remembered as 'pulling the plug' on McCartney.

17 July 2012: Dublin, RDS Arena

Following the 'pull the plug' incident at London, Bruce started his next show in Dublin with a big 'power switch' prop on stage and started with a brief 'Twist And Shout', saying: 'Before we were so rudely interrupted…!' Fittingly, 'I Fought The Law' followed, a tour debut, as was a sign request, 'I'm A Rocker'. Another tour debut, 'My Hometown', was dedicated to U2. During the encores, two stooges dressed as police and a city official tried twice to 'turn the power off' with the big switch, but Bruce and Steve defended it, keeping it 'ON'. 'Easy Money' was performed both nights in Dublin, as Patti was present. Local friend Tom McCormack had a cool sign.

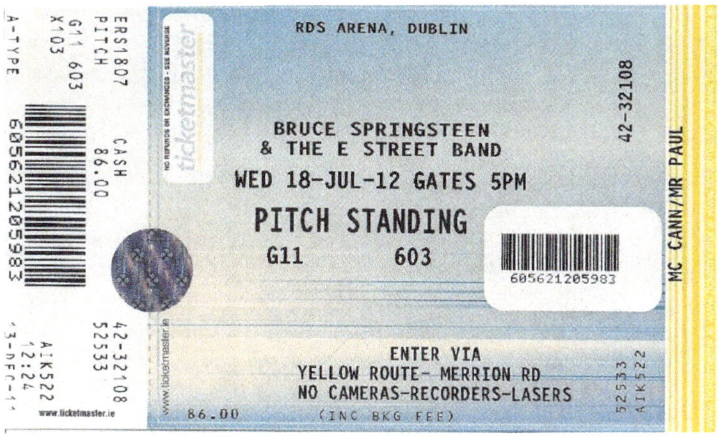

18 July 2012: Dublin, RDS Arena

Jake spent the second Dublin show seated and needed a wheelchair to enter and leave the stage; Bruce explained he'd put his back out. During 'Spirit In The Night', he ad-libbed: 'Crazy Jakey got really hurt, he sneezed, threw out his back in just his socks and shirt!' Sixteen different songs were played, including the opening 'This Hard Land' (solo acoustic), three in a row from 'Darkness On The Edge Of Town', 'Jackson Cage', 'The Promise' (solo piano), 'The River', 'Backstreets', and 'Rocky Ground'. 'What's a curfew?' read one sign.
Many memorable encounters for me in Dublin, including Kevin Buell (thanks Paul) and Liz Clarke.

Kevin Buell photo thanks to Paul McCann

Liz from DC

27 July 2012: Gothenburg, Ullevi

Having soundchecked both 'Girls In Their Summer Clothes' and 'Drive All Night' the first night of two at Gothenburg, Bruce played both tour premieres – the first linked to a request, and the second accompanied by the crowd's mobile phones glowing like 'fireflies' as he recalled summer parties. 'The Promised Land' opened, with four more songs before the usual 'We Take Care Of Our Own' show kick-off, including 'Something In The Night' and 'My Love Will Not Let You Down'. 'Twist And Shout' - the 'stadium breaker' - of course had to be played, and was featured at both concerts.

Thanks to Kezia for my ticket on this date.

28 July 2012: Gothenburg, Ullevi

A steadily wet day prompted Stevie to predict a show 'for the ages' on social media, and it was indeed, starting with some Swedish from Bruce and 'Who'll Stop The Rain'. Between 'Downbound Train' and 'I'm Goin' Down', he called it a 'little "Born In The USA" double hitter'. 'Lost In The Flood' was a request and tour debut; 'It's Hard To Be A Saint In The City' was another request; 'Frankie' (soundchecked) was a third request and a European debut, its first time since 2003. 'Where The Bands Are', its only appearance in 2012, was dedicated to tour-following fans. For the first time since Clarence's death in June 2011, 'Jungleland' was played, and dedicated to him, noting his relationship with Sweden as 'a special place for him' and another home. Once again, stadium breaking was attempted with the final 'Twist And Shout'.

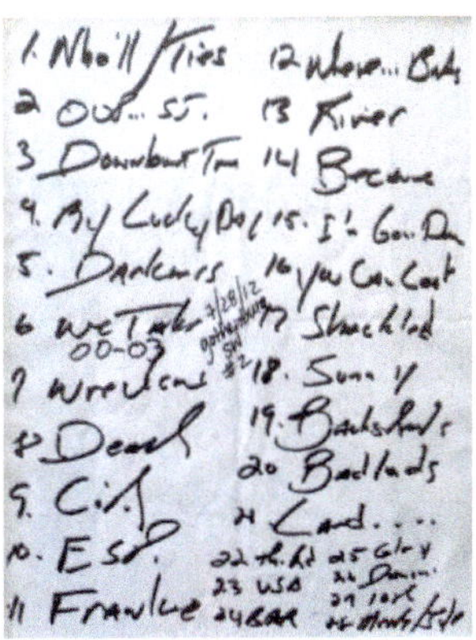

31 July 2012: Helsinki, Olympiastadion

Just as we thought the two Gothenburg shows couldn't be beaten, Bruce surprised everyone at 'the Finnish finish' with the longest show of his career, 33 songs over four hours and almost five minutes, plus a five-song solo acoustic pre-show for early comers. I was buying rolls for Mike and Jim and hearing the pre-show begin, had to rush back. Having met fans at the front and arranged request signs around the drums, Bruce started the main set with Fogerty's 'Rockin' All Over The World'. Highlights included 'Prove It All Night' (with '78 intro), a rare 'Light Of Day' (by request), 'Back In Your Arms' (tour debut and request), and 'Detroit Medley'. Stevie duetted with Bruce on a request for his 'I Don't Want To Go Home', not played since 1981. The last European debut was '(Your Love Keeps Lifting Me) Higher And Higher'; Jon Landau guested on guitar for this and the closer 'Twist And Shout', which took the show over the four-hour mark. Big thanks to the 'This Hard Land' fan club for superb help to all.

29 April 2013: Oslo, Telenor Arena

Follow That Dream: Helen and I planned to follow most of the Nordic part of the 2013 leg, and blew a big part of our food budget on the first hotel breakfast in pricey Oslo (almost £50 each – we skipped lunch). Bruce did a four-song solo acoustic pre-show for us early die-hards (including Thomas & Franky, and Connor) – including Bruce's only European performance of 'The Fever'. Stevie, newly returned to the band after filming 'Lilyhammer', opened the main show as his Frank Tagliano character doing a relocated 'My Kind Of Town'. The soundchecked 'Follow That Dream' made its tour debut.

'Little Thomas' & Franky

30 April 2013: Oslo, Telenor Arena

Bruce made fifteen setlist changes for the second night in Oslo, including a soundchecked 'Leap Of Faith' to open. Other variations were 'Downbound Train', 'Cover Me', 'Open All Night', a request for 'Savin' Up', and 'The Promise' (solo piano). Also in the soundcheck was 'Shout', this set's finale, which would soon feature fairly frequently in the last encores.

Monika (in purple 'Stevie' top) joins the 'Dancing In The Dark' guests

ticnet
ticketmaster Sverige
This is your ticket
see full purchase policy on ticnet.se
TicketFast
LIVE NATION
PROUDLY PRESENTS
BRUCE SPRINGSTEEN
& THE E STREET BAND
FRIENDS ARENA, SOLNA-STOCKHOLM
FREDAG 3 MAJ 2013 KL. 19.30
PARKETT STÅPLATS
GATE 1
NO CAMERAS, RECORDERS OR LASER POINTERS
ÅLDERSGRÄNS 13 ÅR PGA LJUDNIVÅ
Dissmann,Ralf
CUSTOMER NO: 4510913
ORDER NO: 11982761
Ordinarie
AMOUNT: 650.00 kr
SERVICE FEE: 45.00 kr
December 7,2012 09:10
FDS
ORD
UOWC5+PU
(c) 2012 Ticketmaster All rights reserved

3 May 2013: Stockholm, Friends Arena

Thanks to Ralf for my ticket for the first of three indoor Friends Arena concerts at Solna, an area north of Stockholm. Bruce recognised the band's historical relationship with Sweden, announcing they were going to do something special – I assumed a single rare song – and was floored when he said they would play the 'Born To Run' album from start to finish, the first time any Springsteen album had been played live in sequence in Europe; in the US, such plans were previously declared in advance. Because of this, the usual pause during 'Tenth Avenue Freeze-Out' was (permanently) skipped, although the memorial slideshow was shown during the last part. 'Mountain Of Love' was an acoustic request performance, and Elliott Murphy joined in for 'Glory Days'.

Elliott Murphy guested for 'Glory Days' at Stockholm

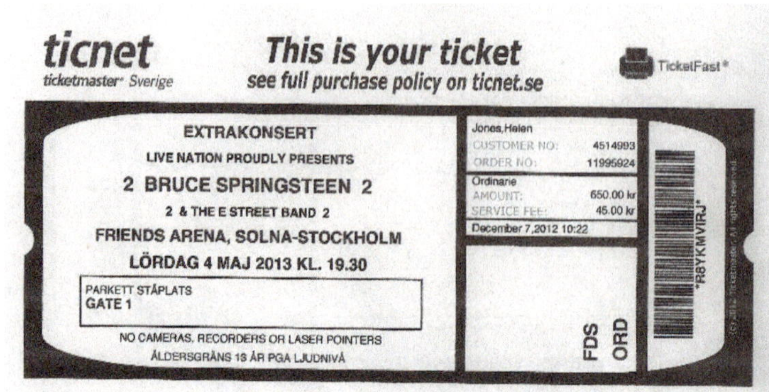

4 May 2013: Stockholm, Friends Arena

Opening with 'My Love Will Not Let You Down', a request early in the set was 'I'm A Rocker'. 'Leap Of Faith' and 'Better Days' were two nods to the 'Lucky Town' album. A further 'special gift' for Sweden was in store, when Bruce announced they would play another album in full for the second night (Soozie's birthday): 'Darkness On The Edge Of Town'. Having chased it since my first Springsteen concerts in 1981, I finally got to hear 'Streets Of Fire' live, the rarest track from the album. When the sequence was complete, the core band members came forward for a bow before the show continued.

Friends at Friends Arena: Big Neil and Brother Jim, Stockholm

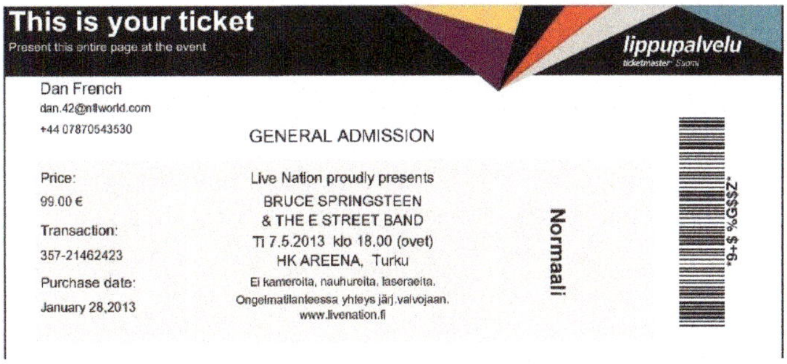

7 May 2013: Turku, HK Areena

Instead of a single larger concert at Helsinki, Finland was treated to two more intimate concerts at Turku's 12,000 capacity HK Areena, and Bruce really played mostly to the cosy pit, recognising the local fan club 'This Hard Land' with that song. 'Brilliant Disguise' and 'Queen Of The Supermarket' (by request) were audible rarities, and our new local friend Salla – one of those working hard helping organise the fan lines – played guitar onstage during 'Dancing In The Dark', rocking her moment – still my proudest stage photo from a Bruce show. My two favourite 2013 shows also. Go, Salla!

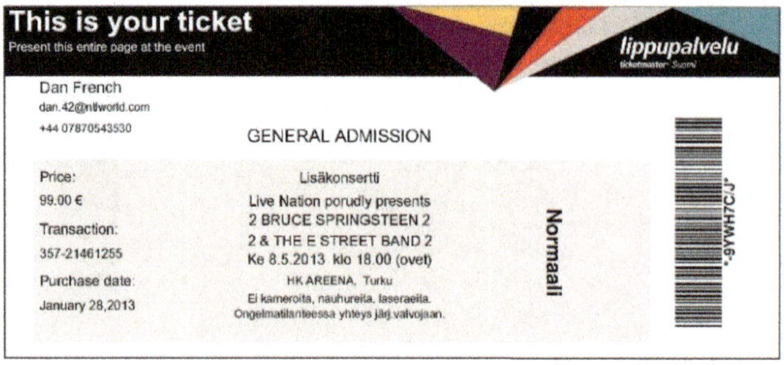
This is your ticket
Present this entire page at the event
lippupalvelu
ticketmaster Suomi
Dan French
dan.42@ntlworld.com
+44 07870543530
GENERAL ADMISSION
Price:
99.00 €
Transaction:
357-21461255
Purchase date:
January 28,2013
Lisäkonsertti
Live Nation porudly presents
2 BRUCE SPRINGSTEEN 2
2 & THE E STREET BAND 2
Ke 8.5.2013 klo 18.00 (ovet)
HK AREENA, Turku
Ei kameroita, nauhureita, laseraeita.
Ongelmatilanteessa yhteys järj.valvojaan.
Normaali
-9YWH7C/J

8 May 2013: Turku, HK Areena

'Nicholas from Belgium' had a long-standing dream fulfilled when he met Bruce before the second Turku show with his request sign for 'Wages Of Sin' which he'd brought to many shows over several tours. The band rehearsed it thoroughly at the soundcheck, the unique performance was dedicated to Nicholas at the show, and it was later issued as an official video. The opening solo acoustic 'I'll Work For Your Love' seemed a nod to the 2012 Helsinki pre-show version. 'Ain't Good Enough For You', 'Open All Night' and 'Racing In The Street' were Finnish debuts, and 'The River' was dedicated to Pere Cairó, Connor's teacher friend from Barcelona, who had died in 2012.

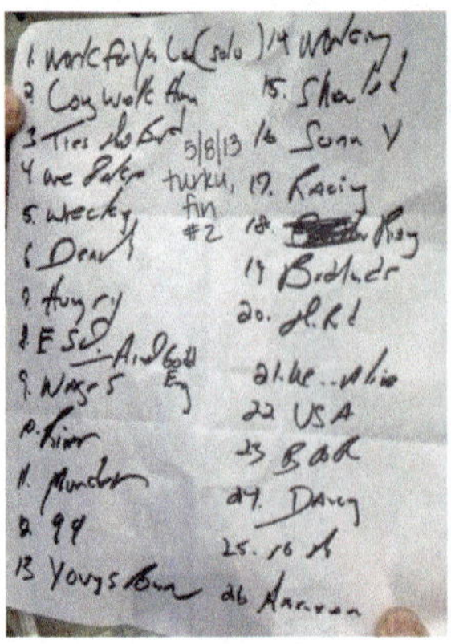

Dedication rewarded: Nicholas finally got his wish, 'Wages Of Sin'

11 May 2013: Stockholm, Friends Arena

The third 2013 Swedish show, after the Finland break, featured another full album set: 'Born In The USA'. Up first was 'The Promised Land', and the traditional 'stadium breaker' 'Twist And Shout' finished the concert again.

Thanks message to Sweden from Bruce and the E Street Band

This is your ticket
Present this entire page at the event

Live Nation billetnet

Dan French
INNER PITCH - STÅ
Entrance A6A

Event code: PAR1405
Customer number: 3488656
Order number: 10364247
Purchase date: 10. December, 2012

Bruce Springsteen & The E Street Band
Tuesday, 14 May, 2013 at 20:00
Parken
Øster Allé 50
2100 København Ø
Ingen garderobe
Koncerten er under tag
Dørene åbnes kl. 18:00

Price: 650,00 kr
Fee: 20,00 kr
Total: 670,00 kr
PLK
Standard

KOH-HLWS4

14 May 2013: Copenhagen, Parken

Jon Landau's birthday show, and he guested again, for 'Twist And Shout'. No less than four sign requests in a row: 'Loose Ends', 'Cadillac Ranch' (thanks Sören), 'Radio Nowhere' and 'Trapped', soon before the full 'Born To Run' album in sequence. Anne was among fans meeting Bruce at his hotel, her priceless reaction captured by local press. It was also Connor's first time meeting Bruce, and meeting Luba (who'd have her 'For You' request played at the next show). We heard Bruce soundchecking 'Highway Patrolman' from outside. The end of my 2013 Nordic eight-show mini-tour.

Anne Simonsen reacting to her Bruce encounter, Copenhagen
Photo thanks to Katrine Emilie Andersen for B.T.

Connor meets his hero in Copenhagen – photo thanks to Anne Simonsen

Connor and Luba

Connor's happy place – the central stage podium, Copenhagen

Jon Landau guesting at Copenhagen – photo by Connor Kirkpatrick

26 May 2013: Munich, Olympiastadion

The memory of Munich still gives me a chill – despite being late May, an extreme combination of the coldest, wettest, windiest conditions together at a Bruce show for me; there were reports of snow at the local airport. I should have done as Ralf did and shelter in the hotel, but instead opted for major exposure (almost hypothermia) waiting in line. Big thanks to my fellow sufferers for the distraction of their company – as Brenda dubbed us, the International Group! I hoped that when we got into the stadium, it would offer some shelter, but having taken up my usual back of the pit position, the elements were right in my face! The first time I seriously considered leaving before a Bruce show. I only took one photo during the show, as – like Bruce - my hands were so cold: a clever wearable two-sided sign modelled by a young boy, Tom. Bruce played both songs: 'Seaside Bar Song' and 'Rosalita (Come Out Tonight)', the latter unusually early in the set. The full 'Born In The USA' album was clearly an attempt to warm everyone up. A Facebook support group still exists!

The International Group

An ingenious wearable two-sided sign

15 June 2013: London, Wembley Stadium

A full performance of the 'Darkness On The Edge Of Town' album for London ('a record of songs that still form the centre of who we are and what we do and of our set each night'), as Bruce played the new Wembley Stadium for the first time. He dropped the planned solo opener 'The Ghost Of Tom Joad', but did play the soundchecked 'Jackson Cage' and 'Save My Love'. The latter, plus 'Rosalita (Come Out Tonight)' and 'Lost In The Flood' were all sign requests; he closed with a solo acoustic 'Thunder Road'.

18 June 2013: Glasgow, Hampden Park

The first show played on an anniversary of Clarence's death, and the Big Man was much in our thoughts at Glasgow. Rarities included 'It's Hard To Be A Saint In The City', 'Jolé Blon' and 'Spirit In The Night'; and a three-pack from 'Nebraska': 'Atlantic City', 'Johnny 99' and 'Open All Night'. 'Thunder Road' was the final song, solo acoustic. About two-thirds of the setlist were songs not previously played in Scotland. The ticket mentioned the 23.00 curfew time.

Big Neil, family and friends in the pit

20 June 2013: Coventry, Ricoh Arena

Helen's 150th show! An enterprising cider seller delivered Swedish cider to us in the queue – very civilised. Bruce started with a solo acoustic 'The Ghost Of Tom Joad' as setlisted, and in response to a 'Play Anything' sign request did 'Two Hearts'. 'Seeds', 'Trapped' and 'The River' were also sign requests, as was the first full E Street Band version of 'Long Time Comin'', rehearsed two days earlier. Full 'Born To Run' album show, for James Gandolfini. One sign asked 'Bruce! Can I Have A Man Hug', and Bruce did so, assuring the young guy – who'd been dumped – that he'd be OK.

29 June 2013: Paris, Stade De France

I bumped into Caroline on her own at the same hotel, and having heard our friend Beverly had unfortunately been mugged nearby, we hung out together for solidarity; the Stade De France area didn't seem welcoming after that news.

In the pit at Paris, I said to Caroline: 'It feels like a pre-show kind of day'. Minutes later, Bruce strolled on with acoustic guitar and played 'This Hard Land', 'Burning Love' and 'Growin' Up'. 'How did you know?' asked Caroline; 'No idea, just a random feeling…' I replied. Three songs in to the main set, Bruce reacted to a 'Lucille' sign request: 'Someone is trying to stump the E Street Band already!' 'Born In The USA' was played in full during the show, and for 'Pay Me My Money Down' percussionist Everett Bradley played a washboard. Elliott Murphy with son Gaspard both guested on 'Born To Run'. Souvenir cups were on sale, and some got discarded, finding a good home.

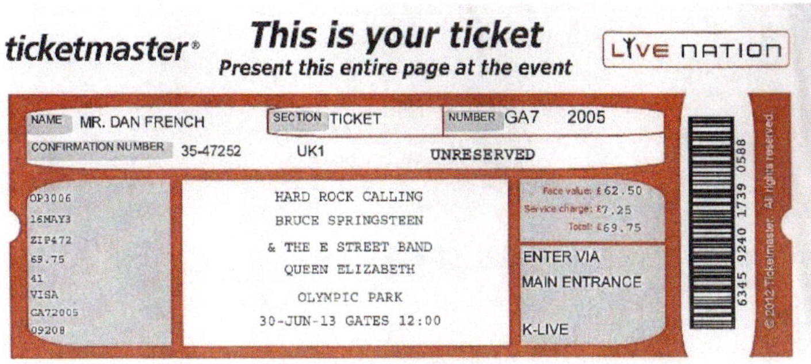
ticketmaster®
This is your ticket
Present this entire page at the event
LIVE NATION

NAME MR. DAN FRENCH
SECTION TICKET
NUMBER GA7 2005
CONFIRMATION NUMBER 35-47252
UK1
UNRESERVED

OP3006
16MAY3
ZIP472
69.75
41
VISA
CA72005
09208

HARD ROCK CALLING
BRUCE SPRINGSTEEN
& THE E STREET BAND
QUEEN ELIZABETH
OLYMPIC PARK
30-JUN-13 GATES 12:00

Face value: £62.50
Service charge: £7.25
Total: £69.75
ENTER VIA
MAIN ENTRANCE
K-LIVE

6345 9240 1739 0588
© 2012 Ticketmaster. All rights reserved.

30 June 2013: London, Hard Rock Calling

After the plug-pulling fiasco at the end of Hard Rock Calling in 2012, some expected Bruce would boycott any return – perhaps the shift in venue from Hyde Park to the Queen Elizabeth Olympic Park helped sell the idea. Somehow we ended up with some passes for the guest area, and had time to visit there early on.The festival line-up included Alabama Shakes, and Jake was spotted side stage checking their set out. Three 'Nebraska' songs together included two by request: 'Johnny 99' and 'Reason To Believe', before 'Atlantic City'. 'Born In The USA' was played as a full album sequence again, Bruce perhaps assuming nobody would have rushed from the previous day's show in Paris to be there as well! His mother and sister were on stage, Pamela playing guitar on 'Dancing In The Dark'. Zac Brown (also on the bill) joined in on 'Tenth Avenue Freeze-Out'. Instead of a solo acoustic 'Thunder Road' to finish, Bruce got distracted by a young fan with tattoos and played an acoustic 'My Lucky Day', joking about how he felt too old for tattoos but still appreciated them.

20 July 2013: Belfast, King's Hall

Having caught Bruce's first ever Belfast show indoors in 1996, this time it was outdoors at the same King's Hall complex. Ticket thanks to Paul M again. Some fine signs, such as Salla's cool hope for 'Janey Needs A Shooter' – 11 years ahead of its time! 'Surprise, Surprise' was appropriate as the first of a 5-song acoustic pre-show, with 'Maria's Bed', 'Growin' Up', 'In Dreams' (a sign asked for Roy Orbison's 'California Blue', which Bruce said he couldn't play), and 'This Hard Land'. 'This Little Light Of Mine' was played to start and end the show at this and three other shows between Limerick and Cardiff. Five 'Nebraska' songs done including the title track, a tour premiere; as was 'Fade Away', third time in Europe, for die-hard 'Tom' (Thomas), 'Steve's doppelganger'!

Go Salla! Cool sign *Christina has a proper front-row smooch*

23 July 2013: Cardiff, Millennium Stadium

Cardiff, with its roof closed, was set up as a part-stadium, creating a more intimate indoor arena effect. A request sign prompted the still unique premiere of 'TV Movie', followed by the European debut of 'Cynthia'. Mid-show, Eric Burdon guested on The Animals' 'We Gotta Get Out Of This Place', not played since 1976; and 'Boom Boom' and 'Summertime Blues' added to the rarities list. During 'Shout', a particularly loose Bruce didn't just get down low as normal, but crawled right down the front of the stage. Unusually, Bruce played a pair of solo acoustic songs after the band had finished with the repeated 'This Little Light Of Mine' again: 'Janey, Don't You Lose Heart' and 'Thunder Road'.

At three and a half hours and 33 songs, released as part of the Nugs live archive series, Cardiff remains a favourite Bruce concert for many, both from 2013 and overall.

24 July 2013: Leeds, Leeds Arena

The day after Cardiff, Leeds needed a quick journey to cover both cities (thanks again to Helen). Unofficially opening the new 13,000 capacity indoor arena, Bruce tickets here were among the toughest of the tour. Our friend Holly (RIP), working for Soozie, helped many fans with tickets during her mid-July visit. The printed setlist bizarrely showed the first side of 'The Wild, The Innocent & The E Street Shuffle' in sequence, not played. The show still held many surprises, starting with 'Roulette' and soon including 'Local Hero' with a new horn arrangement, immediately followed by the soundchecked 'Gotta Get That Feeling' (European debut), then 'Bad Moon Rising', and 'Thundercrack' (both UK debuts). A very rare 'This Depression' made only its seventh appearance ever. Also soundchecked, 'Secret Garden' (another European premiere) was dedicated to hard-core fans following the tour, especially 'Annie and her guy' (Jeff).

Connor's promise from Jake eventually happened at Galway in 2015

27 July 2013: Kilkenny, Nowlan Park

Dubbed the 'Wrecking Ball Weekender', Bruce headlined two shows at Kilkenny supported by different musicians each night: firstly Josh Ritter, Damien Dempsey, and Glen Hansard. Gordon brought a giant Irish greeting card for signing, and distributed a large number of green 'THANK YOU' sheets to be held up for Bruce in the show. 'Shake' and 'Sweet Soul Music' were both sign requests and tour debuts early in the set; other rarities included 'Stand On It', 'Long Time Comin'' and 'Jack Of All Trades'. This concert featured the full 'Born In The USA' album in sequence, and during the encores, Glen Hansard joined the band to guest on 'Drive All Night', throwing in a line or two of 'Here Comes The Night' mid-song.

Gordon's big card being signed

Kilkenny says THANK YOU!

28 July 2013: Kilkenny, Nowlan Park

'The older you get, the more it means': Thanks to Paul for my tickets both days. The weekender continued, supported by Delorentos, LAPD and Imelda May. A full 'Born To Run' album show, with 'a little four-song segment that are some debts I got to pay...' starting with 'The River': 'John, this is for your brother Tom.' Rehearsed and setlisted, 'Wild Billy's Circus Story' (band version European debut) was for Tero; 'Man At The Top' (European debut) for Markus; and 'When You Walk In The Room', played at Hammersmith in 1975 – fittingly for Linda, there with Helen among 'my ladies' Bruce recognised at the front. Ali Weinberg guested in the encores, and the 2013 European tour finished with the same solo acoustic song that had opened it in Oslo: 'This Hard Land'.

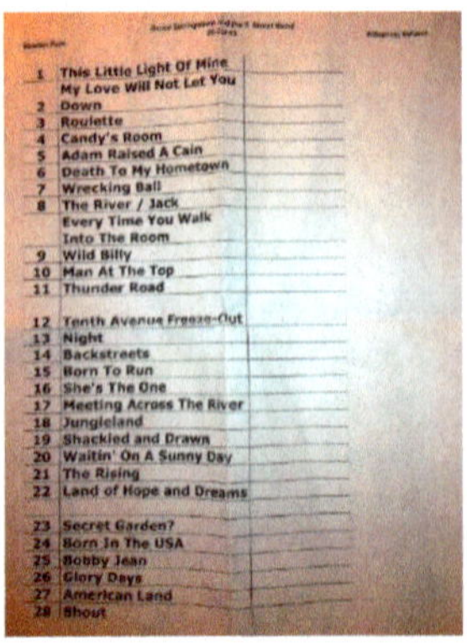
1 This Little Light Of Mine
My Love Will Not Let You
2 Down
3 Roulette
4 Candy's Room
5 Adam Raised A Cain
6 Death To My Hometown
7 Wrecking Ball
8 The River / Jack
Every Time You Walk
Into The Room
9 Wild Billy
10 Man At The Top
11 Thunder Road

12 Tenth Avenue Freeze-Out
13 Night
14 Backstreets
15 Born To Run
16 She's The One
17 Meeting Across The River
18 Jungleland
19 Shackled and Drawn
20 Waitin' On A Sunny Day
21 The Rising
22 Land of Hope and Dreams

23 Secret Garden?
24 Born In The USA
25 Bobby Jean
26 Glory Days
27 American Land
28 Shout

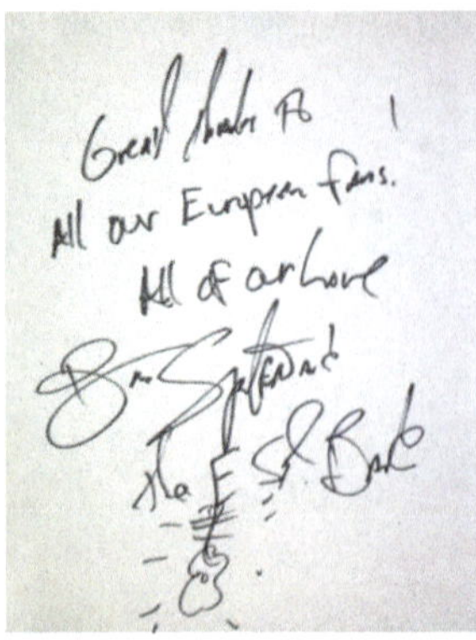

2014

After the *High Hopes* tour

22 May 2014: Pittsburgh, Soldiers & Sailors Memorial Hall & Museum

Bruce with Joe Grushecky & The Houserockers, unusually marked as special guest on the tickets and merchandise. In April 2014, Bruce announced during the Pittsburgh 'High Hopes' concert that he'd be back there for this pair of shows. When the 'High Hopes' tour didn't come to Europe, and I realised how easy it was to get tickets for two nights at this 2,300 seat indoor venue, I was rewarded (both nights) with multiple rarities and great views (I started in Row O in the stalls but got upgraded mid-show by Beverly to much nearer – thanks Bev!). Bruce was on strong medication after a (back?) injury at the recent end of the E Street Band tour, and seemed a little stiff at times, but the setlists easily made up for that, especially 'Racing In The Street ('78)', 'Frankie Fell In Love', 'Hearts Of Stone' and the live premiere of 'Leavin' Train', plus Bruce's solo acoustic performances: 'Mary Queen Of Arkansas', 'Two For The Road', 'Kingdom Of Days', 'The Wall' and 'Incident On 57th Street'. Rick Witkowski guested on guitar during the first night's encores.

Soldiers & Sailors Memorial Hall

Rick Witkowski guested

23 May 2014: Pittsburgh, Soldiers & Sailors Memorial Hall & Museum

Thanks to Beverly again, we ended up even closer to the stage for the second night. ‘One Way Street’ was among the titles soundchecked, but not played. Five solo acoustic songs included ‘Further On (Up The Road)’, ‘I’ll Work For Your Love’, ‘Outlaw Pete’, ‘My Beautiful Reward’ and ‘Jersey Girl’. Bruce jokingly mentioned he was still heavily medicated.

2016

The River 2016 tour

27 January 2016: New York City, Madison Square Garden

On 9 January 2016, I was woken at home in the small hours by Holly calling from New York, offering me the option to buy guest tickets (courtesy of Soozie) to three shows on the upcoming US 'River 2016' tour. At that time no European leg was known, so I jumped at the chance to take in the last three shows in January, teaming up with Deb for Madison Square Garden. Luckily missing Storm Jonas which postponed the previous show, I went straight from the plane to my hotel and then an early dinner with her before we spent some time getting lost and redirected around the Garden, looking for the E Street Lounge, eventually bumping into Tom Cunningham (hi Tom!) coming out of the lounge, and realising it was time to head for the pit anyway. My first 'Meet Me In The City', and at last ticking off 'Crush On You'. Bruce got the intro to 'I Wanna Marry You' wrong and blamed the band at first, before realising it was his fault! He also forgot Garry during the band introductions. A jet-lagged but fun start to the week, indeed…

29 January 2016: Washington DC, Verizon Center

My three-state mini-tour continued to DC, where I had time for a quick lunch and catch-up with old friend Sebla and her husband Steve; she was a pen-pal supporter of my 'Point Blank' fanzine from Turkey in the 1980s. Also great to bump into other local friends Liz and Magnus during and after the show. Thanks to Christy for a whistle-stop car tour of the sights, adding Virginia to my list of US states visited.

Following the 'River' album sequence, Bruce played four tour debuts together: 'Darlington County', 'Prove It All Night', 'The Promised Land', and 'Tougher Than The Rest'. First encore 'No Surrender' was dedicated to the Vietnam Veterans, Bobby Muller, and Ryan Chalmers. I had time while in the city to pay my own respects at the Vietnam Veterans Memorial wall, and see other nearby monuments for the first time.

Sebla – photo thanks to Steve

31 January 2016: Newark, Prudential Center

The third of my January 2016 shows thanks to Holly, with Connor. Bruce dedicated a late 'Badlands' to the Community Food Bank of New Jersey, for whom our host Molly was volunteering. A nightmare getting into the building, due to a raucous crowd and over-zealous security staff delaying entry, but eventually we got a spot by the left side of the pit – well located for a 'low-five' hand slap from Bruce. His son Sam was nearby with guests, and Connor took a picture over my shoulder making it look like we were ignoring each other (Sam was ignoring me, unsurprisingly)! After the full 'River' album segment, Bruce played 'Lonesome Day', 'Working On The Highway' and 'Atlantic City' for the first time that year.

'Blanked' by Sam!
Photo by Connor Kirkpatrick

Bruce 'low-fives' one hand while
I snap the pic with the other

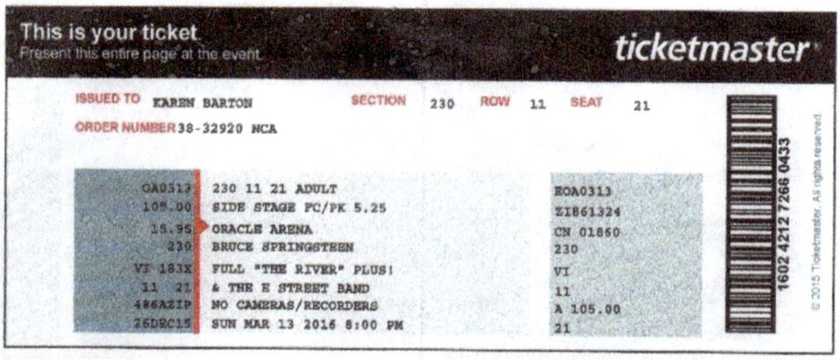

13 March 2016: Oakland, Oracle Arena

My flight to San Francisco was delayed a day by fog in Dublin, and my hold baggage went missing (it returned home after a longer trip than me, via Boston), but luckily, I made it with time to spare on show day – thanks to Beverly for accommodation and t-shirt loans, and to Paul for welcome company in Dublin! My ticket came from Karen (thanks 'Sammy') and after the travel hassles, I was glad just to sit and take it in. A relief also to hang out with Janice on arrival; and looking at my photos later, there was Oliver in the pit. 'Checkered Shirt Guy' Steven not only had his 'Growin' Up' request played, but got invited up to sing with Bruce – he really seized his moment!

Oliver snapped in the pit

'Checkered Shirt Guy' Steven at top

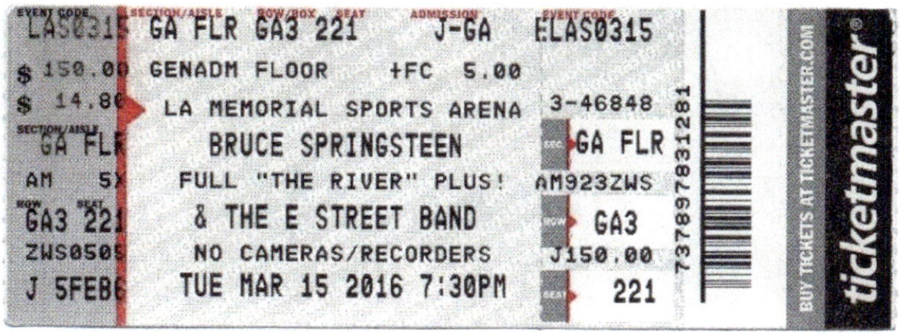

15 March 2016: Los Angeles, Los Angeles Memorial Sports Arena

The first of three shows in LA closing down ‘The Dump That Jumps’. I flew from San Francisco with Beverly, and was based with her, Janice, Graham and José at The Hotel California in Santa Monica. Mike, Neil and Gordon joined us via the Badlands group (including the legendary Bernie), and it was a joyful rendezvous with Sammy and Dari at the shows. Annette and Mel went with Sammy, Mike and I for a custom car tour of Hollywood sights, and a fab group meal afterwards.

Sly Stallone was among the local celebrities present, applauded by the audience nearby. Souvenir cups and other signage for the three-night stand read ‘The Dump That Jumps Is Going Out In Style’.

Hotel California gang: Janice, Graham, Beverly and José

Gordon, Sammy, Dari and Neil – photo thanks to Mike

17 March 2016: Los Angeles, Los Angeles Memorial Sports Arena

The second of three Los Angeles shows was St Patrick's Day, and Bruce rehearsed 'American Land' and 'Death To My Hometown' at the soundcheck, which both featured in the set as tour premieres after the full 'River' album portion of the concert. It was a family event, with guests including Jason and Madison Federici, Jarod Clemons, and Olivia Tallent all joining in for 'Tenth Avenue Freeze-Out'; Madison also danced during 'Dancing In The Dark'.

Stevie feels the Irish spirit

Clemons cousins: Jake and Jarod

19 March 2016: Los Angeles, Los Angeles Memorial Sports Arena

The third concert at Los Angeles was added after the first two, meaning some friends had already booked their flights home and it wasn't economical to change them. A few of us extended our stays and caught the final night before the venue was closed and torn down; appropriately, Bruce added references to Los Angeles for 'Wrecking Ball'. The show was 3 hours and 43 minutes; the lengthening trend would continue during the year. A sign reading 'Dancing Is A Man's Job' got a male fan on stage for 'Dancing In The Dark'. Alex Bittan and Harley Federici joined the previous night's family guests for the last two encores before 'Bobby Jean'.

21 May 2016: Madrid, Estadio Santiago Bernabeu

The last of three times Bruce played at the Bernabeu stadium since 2008, and my first visit to the Spanish city. I wasn't very well for the shows I saw in May, so some mixed memories. Two social highlights were Ekaterina introducing me to Steven 'Checkered Shirt Guy' Strauss, continuing his marathon run of shows that tour; and meeting Winni again. There was a bizarre moment waiting in line outside the venue, trying to listen to Bruce soundchecking while an oblivious fan was serenading the line with acoustic Bruce covers at the same time as the real thing was playing live inside! Two soundchecked tour debuts at Madrid were 'My City Of Ruins' and 'Land Of Hope And Dreams', and 'Trapped' was a successful sign request. The final song was a solo acoustic 'Thunder Road', the first time for that arrangement in 2016.

Ekaterina and Steven

A heartfelt sign asking for help

25 May 2016: Manchester, Etihad Stadium

Unsurprisingly, it was raining again in Manchester, and I was already under the weather. Luckily for me, Magda looked after me, and thankfully we were in sheltered seats together rather than having to stand.

I don't recall very much of the show except that it was famous as the time that Santa Claus came to Manchester in May! Bruce spotted a fan in a Santa suit in the crowd, and with much amusement asked if there was any connection between Manchester and Santa Claus or if it was 'a perverted attempt at a request of some sort'. The 'Manchester Santa' duly got invited up to the stage ('You can't be shy; you've got the Santa suit on') and guested on 'Santa Claus Is Comin' To Town'. ('Nobody knew that Manchester was where Santa lives in the off season – now we know…')

Bruce continued to mention the rain while introducing other songs, checking 'Are the Manchesterians with me?' As he's often said onstage in the face of such weather, he wouldn't have it any other way.

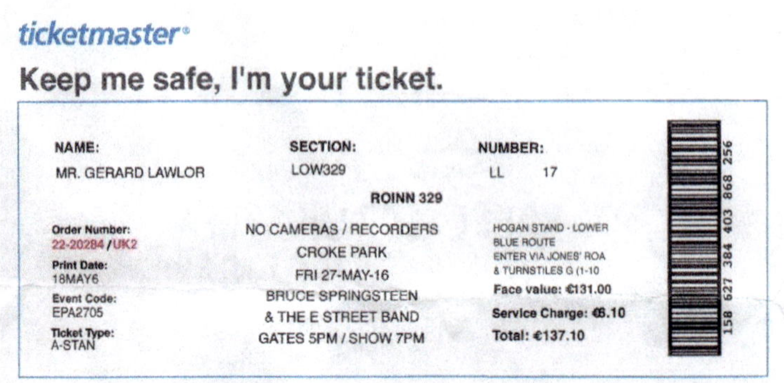
ticketmaster®

Keep me safe, I'm your ticket.

NAME: MR. GERARD LAWLOR

SECTION: LOW329

NUMBER: LL 17

ROINN 329

Order Number: 22-20284/UK2
Print Date: 18MAY6
Event Code: EPA2705
Ticket Type: A-STAN

NO CAMERAS / RECORDERS
CROKE PARK
FRI 27-MAY-16
BRUCE SPRINGSTEEN
& THE E STREET BAND
GATES 5PM / SHOW 7PM

HOGAN STAND - LOWER
BLUE ROUTE
ENTER VIA JONES' ROA
& TURNSTILES G (1-10
Face value: €131.00
Service Charge: €6.10
Total: €137.10

158 627 384 403 868 256

27 May 2016: Dublin, Croke Park

The first of two Dublin shows at the massive Croke Park stadium (80,000 plus), and I was again unwell on the 27th, and unable to manage standing – but rescue came in the form of Tom, who found me and passed on a donated Bruce Funds seated ticket (thanks to Gerard Lawlor). I'd supported the wonderful Bruce Funds previously (go Donna) but never dreamed I'd benefit from the system myself in time of need. So – as the sign below reads – THANK YOU! An extensive soundcheck teased the chance of 'Here Comes The Night', but that was shelved. Rehearsed songs that were played included the opener 'Darkness On The Edge Of Town', 'Roulette', 'Back In Your Arms' and 'Lost In The Flood', the latter two also sign requests, as was 'It's Hard To Be A Saint In The City'. On the European 2016 leg, the previous 'full River plus' billing had evolved to what Sammy called 'River-ish'(!) – part but not all of the double album in sequence.

29 May 2016: Dublin, Croke Park

I made it to the pit as planned for the second Dublin 2016 show, and we were treated to a solo piano version of 'Incident On 57th Street', our appetite whetted by hearing it at soundcheck first. 'Youngstown', also rehearsed, made a full band appearance. After a 'Greetings…' triple-pack, half of 'The River' album was played, interspersed with other songs, as far as 'Point Blank' (a first for Ireland, as was 'Independence Day'). All the members of U2 attended the concert, and for 'Because The Night' Bono guested on stage. Another solo performance bookended the show – 'Thunder Road'. Thanks as so often to Paul for my ticket.

1 June 2016: Glasgow, Hampden Park

Like Slane in 1985, another birthday show for Dave, and the third visit to Hampden Park over the years. We bumped into John and Rob, re-enacting a brief reunion of the final NYC 2000 concert gang. Despite or because of the fine Scottish weather, Bruce started off with the soundchecked 'Waitin' On A Sunny Day'. Having played an early sign request for 'Rosalita (Come Out Tonight)', he dedicated '4th Of July, Asbury Park (Sandy)' – first time on the tour - as 'a "Wild And The Innocent" double-header' - to a man who said it was his wedding song. Another tour debut, also soundchecked, was 'American Skin (41 Shots)'. A day for songs with bracketed titles, it seemed. 'This Hard Land' was the solo acoustic finale.

Birthday boy Dave with John & Rob

3 June 2016: Coventry, Ricoh Arena

For Neil, Dave, Mike and I, our Glasgow – Coventry – London road trip continued with a return to Coventry at the misleadingly named Ricoh 'Arena', actually an outdoor stadium. 'Something In The Night' was a tour premiere, preceded by another tour debut - solo piano 'For You'. Request signs generated three more tour premieres: 'Save My Love' (Bruce joked that almost nobody recognised the 'Darkness…' outtake celebrating a tinny 'squawk box' transistor radio from his youth); 'Travelin' Band' (a one-off that tour, dedicated to a band present on the road to London for their own gig); and 'Seven Nights To Rock'.

Feeling the road trip with Big Neil in the pit

5 June 2016: London, Wembley Stadium

I snapped Connor with his adopted Danish family Bodil, Anne and Carsten outside Wembley – as always, it was a truly international gathering in London. Once again Bruce opened with a solo piano performance, having soundchecked 'Does This Bus Stop At 82nd Street?', the first of three tour premieres. The others were a one-off 'Seeds' and a solo acoustic 'I'll Work For Your Love' – started in the wrong key, but he jokingly persisted that it would be worth the wait when he got it right, encouraged by signs requesting it. With Patti present, Bruce played another request, 'Tougher Than The Rest', approving the 'well-thought-out sign'. He congratulated the audience on the quality of the signs there, such as 'Jake, can I kiss your sax?' and 'Can you kiss my wife's leg better?'

ticketmaster

ULLEVI

Keep me safe, I'm your ticket

LIVE NATION PRESENTS
BRUCE SPRINGSTEEN
AND
THE E STREET BAND
ULLEVI GBG, LÖRDAG 25 JUNI 2016 KL 20.00

Entré GH
Stå Främre barrikad
Onumrerat

NO CAMERAS, RECORDERS OR LASERPOINTERS
Åldersgräns 13 år

Deirdre Houston

Customer number:	6572300
Order number:	19807265
Purchased:	25 februari 2016
Ståplats främre barrikad	
Ticket price:	950,00 kr
Service fee:	45,00 kr
Total price:	995,00 kr

BADTM05NH

25 June 2016: Gothenburg, Ullevi

Traditionally Bruce had played a pair of shows when visiting Gothenburg; in 2016 there were two in June and a return third date in July. Thanks to Deirdre for my first ticket.

At the time, at just under four hours, this was the second-longest Springsteen show after Helsinki 2012. 'The Promise' the solo piano opener, was one of three tour premieres and one-offs: the others were 'Tunnel Of Love' and 'Shackled And Drawn', both soundchecked. About a third of the 'River' album was played throughout the set, including 'Drive All Night'. 'Save My Love' and 'The River' (for Anna from Russia) were requests. Introducing the bookending solo acoustic closer 'Thunder Road', Bruce joked that they had maybe another hour to go still!

Back of the pit: with Astrid and Magda

ticketmaster

ULLEVI

Keep me safe, I'm your ticket

LIVE NATION PRESENTS
2 BRUCE SPRINGSTEEN
AND
THE E STREET BAND 2
ULLEVI GBG, MÅNDAG 27 JUNI 2016 KL 20.00

Entré GH
Stå Främre barrikad
Onumrerat

NO CAMERAS, RECORDERS OR LASERPOINTERS
Åldersgräns 13 år

Dan French

Customer number:	5210695
Order number:	19818039
Purchased:	25 februari 2016

Ståplats främre barrikad

Ticket price:	950,00 kr
Service fee:	45,00 kr
Total price:	995,00 kr

DEJKXYB0J

27 June 2016: Gothenburg, Ullevi

For the second Gothenburg 2016 show, the 'River' album content increased to 10 songs. Seventeen titles were changed from the first night, making fifty-five different songs over the two setlists. Bruce soundchecked 'Who'll Stop The Rain', 'Into The Fire' and 'Mary's Place', and began the concert with the latter song as one of three tour premieres. The others were also sign requests: 'Jolé Blon' (with some uncertainty about the key before starting) and 'Lucky Town' ('Haven't played this one in a while'). In the band introductions during 'Shout', Bruce noted that Nils had received an award for 'Swedish-American of the Year'. Finishing with a solo acoustic 'This Hard Land', he repeated the sentiment that 'This is a special place for us, it's a special audience here in Gothenburg and here in Sweden; you've been with us for so long, we appreciate your long support of our music.'

3 July 2016: Milan, Stadio Guiseppe Meazza (San Siro)

Another rough night meant I wasn't in great shape with little energy for my first time at San Siro, but luckily, I'd planned seats both nights for the best view of the fans, very much part of the show. It was a fun and unique moment to be part of the giant welcoming 'Dreams Are Alive Tonite' mosaic organised by the 'Our Love Is Real' group to be held up by fans at the end of the stadium opposite the stage, and Bruce and band were clearly impressed seeing this on their arrival. There were a huge number of coloured signs held up in the pit too. Bruce rewarded the faith of Italian fans with a solo acoustic pre-show song, 'Growin' Up'. The 'River' album was represented by fourteen songs, a further increase. 'Lucille' was a sign request, tour debut and one-off for 2016.

5 July 2016: Milan, Stadio Guiseppe Meazza (San Siro)

'Meet Me In The City' had its European debut to open the second night at Milan, and I was delighted to get a rare performance and the tour premiere of 'Streets Of Fire'. This night, the local fans had organised a second display in the seats opposite the stage – this time using phone lights to spell out a giant 'ESB' prefixed by a heart symbol.

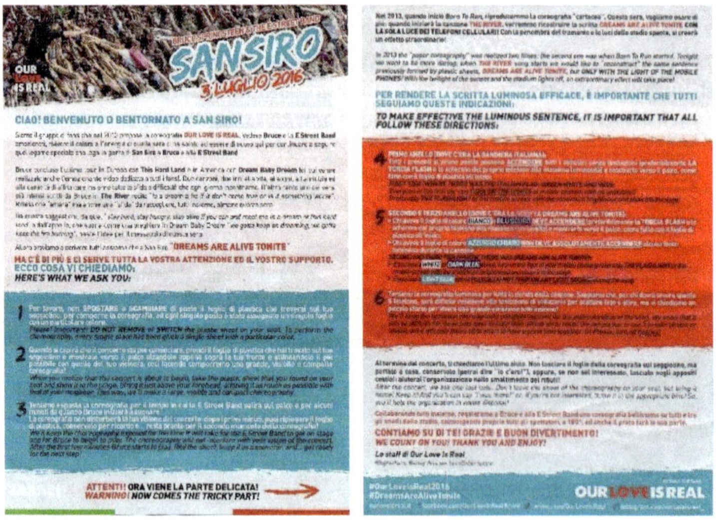

A mosaic instruction flyer from the 'Our Love Is Real' fan group

11 July 2016: Paris, AccorHotels Arena

The former Bercy arena, as well as being a welcome indoor venue, also provided seats behind the stage, offering a unique perspective, more like the band's eye view. This was especially useful when there was a power cut during 'Ramrod', making for a bizarrely extended middle section as Bruce led the unamplified but still playing band around the pit. He then sat on a monitor and signed items for nearby fans while the crew conferred. With power restored and safety checks done, the song and show re-started, and Bruce joked with Stevie: 'Is it fuse-blowing time?' Elliott and Gaspard Murphy guested during 'Born To Run'; rarities included a solo piano 'Incident On 57th Street', 'Reason To Believe' (sung with bullet mic), 'Into The Fire' and 'Nebraska'.

Signing for fans during the power cut

Big Neil & Chris Hunt

13 July 2016: Paris, AccorHotels Arena

In Paris, we met old friend and ex-pat Chris Hunt, (as it turned out, for the last time - RIP) and enjoyed the Bercy 'village' area. Someone had the idea for us to estimate how many Bruce shows we'd seen between us since 1975, and around the table it totalled about 1,046! The third ever airing and European debut of 'Iceman' was a surprise opener (thanks to Pam for her lucky sign), and soon the show marked the first European performance of the full 'River' album in sequence. During 'I Wanna Marry You', Bruce 'married' a fan couple in response to their sign request: 'Mr & Mrs Rock'n'Roll!' The previous show's blown fuse was much referenced, as this time 'Ramrod' went without incident. Repairing to our favourite café in Bercy afterwards, we marvelled at the energy, skill and humour of Djemel, surely the most entertaining waiter in Paris, as he effortlessly coordinated a rapid flow of beers and chips to our table. 'Merci Bercy!'

1,046 shows and counting!

'Merci Bercy!' Djemel the waiter

ticketmaster

ULLEVI

Keep me safe, I'm your ticket

LIVE NATION PRESENTS
BRUCE SPRINGSTEEN
AND
THE E STREET BAND
ULLEVI GBG, LÖRDAG 23 JULI 2016 KL 20.00

Entré GH
Stå Främre barrikad
Onumrerat

NO CAMERAS, RECORDERS OR LASERPOINTERS
Åldersgräns 13 år

Jos Westenberg

Customer number:	1408949
Order number:	19893527
Purchased:	7 mars 2016
Ståplats	
Ticket price:	950,00 kr
Service fee:	45,00 kr
Total price:	995,00 kr

F-T4W/H.8

23 July 2016: Gothenburg, Ullevi

Thanks to Jos for my ticket for the third date at Gothenburg, a month after the first two concerts. Even without the novelty of those June shows, this extra event gathered the usual massive publicity in local papers and media. It was certainly newsworthy: local fans organised a giant 'mosaic' sign right across both levels of the main side seats, displaying the heartfelt message: 'Welcome Home'. Although no doubt planned in advance, it felt like a reward for such long-term loyalty and devotion when the full 'River' album was played in sequence - for the first time outdoors anywhere, after the indoor performance at Paris in mid-July (A third full performance would soon follow in 2016 at Oslo). It was heralded by the Swedish live debut of 'Meet Me In The City' up first. For once, Bruce didn't finish the concert with a solo acoustic song, but instead left it after the 35th song, inevitably the legendary 'stadium breaker': 'Twist And Shout'.

2017

The *Summer '17* tour

2 February 2017: Melbourne, AAMI Park

I'd never been to Australia, but had made friends with other Springsteen fans down under, so when Bruce announced the 'Summer '17' Antipodean leg, Graham – ex-pat from Scotland – invited me with the promise of a ticket, I was sorely tempted, but doubtful I could manage time off work for a trip. Graham persisted, over a few days offering me a second ticket for another show, and then another, and yet another; including help with transport and accommodation, making the idea more enticing each time. It was the fifth ticket offer – after two Melbourne and two Sydney shows – for the legendary Hanging Rock (site of the classic film) that cracked my effort to responsibly resist, and to my delighted surprise my boss Paul said it was too good an opportunity to miss, and agreed I could have some extra unpaid leave. With accommodation and flights falling into place, suddenly an unexpected bonus trip was on!

My five-show tour started in Melbourne, coincidentally also my 200th Springsteen show; what a memorable way to celebrate that landmark number. I joined Graham, Cameron, Robin and other friends in my preferred spot at the back of the pit – connecting with US friends Brenda and Anne nearby too. Unusually, there was a support band on the tour – the reformed Jet. Seeing music stands set up on the riser behind Roy, the expectation was for 'New York City Serenade' to open accompanied by a local string section, as Bruce had often done at recent 2016-2017 shows; and this was a song I'd been chasing forever. My plan was just to watch and listen to this first time – no photos or videos - but I was caught out as Bruce started the show with a solo acoustic cover (and one-off) of 'Don't Hang Up', a '60s song by The Orlons, as an apology on behalf of America to the news that Donald Trump had hung up on a call to the Australian Prime Minister. A quick scramble to video this rarity, followed by uncertainty as the show continued – what happened to 'Serenade'? After nine songs, it was a huge relief when the 8-piece Australian Urban Orchestra took their places, and finally, a sublime 'New York City Serenade' made the long flight so worthwhile.

4 February 2017: Melbourne, AAMI Park

A double support for the second Melbourne show: Jet again, joined by Diesel. American resistance was still on Bruce's mind, as the band started with 'American Land'. A sign request brought a Max fan onstage in 'Out In The Street' to dance by the drum riser. My second experience of 'New York City Serenade', again several songs into the set. I snapped a quick photo of the screen during 'My City Of Ruins' which got a fair amount of attention online with references to 'Blue Shirt Day', although arguably Bruce's shirt was white and just looked blue in the lights. He had trouble getting 'Waitin' On A Sunny Day' going, eventually helped by the crowd. Before 'Born To Run' Bruce encouraged support for the Feed Melbourne Appeal, and using an earlier pit survey, going on to list many countries whose fans travelled to see him – I think Brenda represented Morocco, her work base at the time!

'Blue shirt': during 'My City Of Ruins', Melbourne, 4 February 2017

7 February 2017: Sydney, Qudos Bank Arena

Bruce moved indoors for the two Sydney shows, with 'New York City Serenade' (soundchecked) reverting to set opener, and a request sign prompting a rare cover of 'Long Tall Sally'.

9 February 2017: Sydney, Qudos Bank Arena

My fourth and final 'New York City Serenade' of the trip (twice outdoors, twice indoors) – always mesmerising. Tour debuts: 'Rendezvous' and 'Be True', 'Adam Raised A Cain' and the 'Detroit Medley'. Bruce endorsed the Foodbank of New South Wales while introducing 'Born To Run'. He'd been using a James Brown-style cape reading 'Boss' during 'Shout'.

11 February 2017: Mt Macedon, Hanging Rock

Jet and Diesel were back supporting again as the tour returned outdoors to the spectacular setting of Hanging Rock. Before the show, the main stage screen showed the actual backdrop of the mountain behind. 'The Promised Land' (solo acoustic) was up first, and soon a triple-play from 'Greetings': 'Growin' Up' (referencing a rainbow visible), 'Blinded By The Light' (dedicated to local promoter Michael Gudinski's family) and 'Spirit In The Night' as a sign request. Bruce couldn't resist another sign reading 'I'm Goin' Down On Someone Tonight' and played 'I'm Goin' Down'. The food bank mentioned was Oz Harvest, and a solo acoustic 'Thunder Road' bookended the concert. As we drove away, by our car lights we could see wild kangaroos reclaiming their territory. An unforgettable end to a whirlwind series of five shows in Australia for me.

2018

Springsteen On Broadway

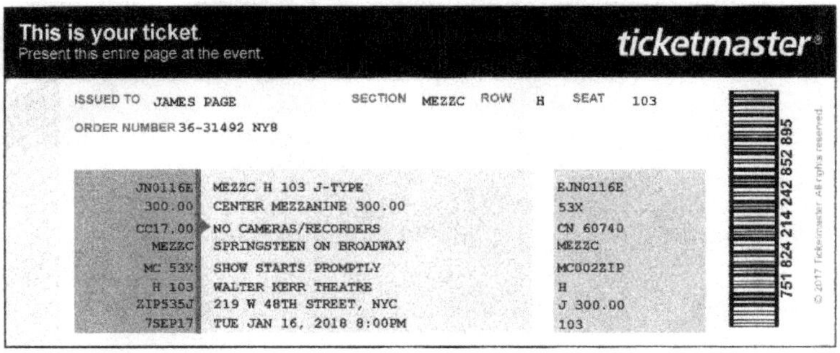

16 January 2018: Walter Kerr Theatre, New York City

I HAVE SEEN THE PAST OF ROCK'N'ROLL, AND ITS NAME IS BRUCE SPRINGSTEEN (ON BROADWAY)*

**with apologies to Jon Landau*

Wow. Just wow. That's all I could write at first about the experience ('show' is too small a word) I had on 16 January. Let me get the superlatives out of the way: amazing, extraordinary, intimate, intense, joyful, emotional, stunning, life-affirming, summational, awe-inspiring, etc, etc – you name it, it challenged description. Expectations were impossibly huge, and although I had soaked up every review I could find, knew what track list to expect, had heard an audio recording of an earlier show, and so I thought I was prepared, I had no idea of the reality. I can't possibly do this justice, and my words here will always feel incomplete, but for those who haven't been or couldn't go, let me try to take you with me...

Walking into the Walter Kerr Theatre, my first reaction was how breathtakingly small and intimate it is. I knew it held 960 seats, and I'd seen photos taken inside, but nothing prepared me for the sense of how small-scaled it looks like in reality. Again, 'wow' was all I could say to my companions, Janice & Molly. I've been lucky enough to see Bruce in small venues before, and immediately I got a sense of how intimate and intense this was going to feel, but at the same time I could tell it would be special in a different way.

Anyone who's been with me to a Bruce Springsteen concert knows my favourite spot is at the back of the pit, where I can relax, see everything fine (for photos and videos) and have space to enjoy the show with other like-minded friends around me. Fittingly, my seat in the theatre was the centre of the back row of the Mezzanine, so at once I felt at home; it was the equivalent of the back of the pit for me. With a well-angled slope of seats ahead, I knew I'd have a perfect view.

8.05pm: showtime. A brief disembodied introduction, and Bruce walked onstage with his acoustic guitar. He launched right away into his spoken 'presentation', for want of a better word. It's not like a concert (although it's talking, music, and quoting from his book), although I have never felt more 'in concert' with Bruce on stage. Jon Landau referred to Bruce's career as a 'conversation' with his fans, but it's so much more than that, it's a RELATIONSHIP, for many of us unlike any other connection we have to our favourite musical artists; and this event is an extremely powerful re-affirmation, concentration and solidification of that relationship. If it was a marriage, it would feel like a renewal of vows. An early review wisely pointed out that previously Bruce's stories have served his songs, but here – and especially vividly in the first part of the night – it was the other way around. This really highlighted how the two forms are not separate but united. 'Singer-songwriter' isn't enough of a title to describe what he does, he's a 'Songwriter-storyteller-singer'. Often the talking was underpinned by gentle musings on guitar or piano. His command of the audience never ceases to amaze me after all these years: there were one or two people who felt the need to whoop or call out now and then, but blessedly few, as this demands attention – apart from natural applause at the end of songs, instinctively it seemed right to wait for Bruce to cue us when it was appropriate to express ourselves, and this totally reinforced the intimacy and effectiveness, drawing us all closer together, hanging on his words. At times I felt as if I'd been holding my breath for much of the two hours and twenty minutes he was on stage.

In addition, of course, Bruce is a masterful musician and performer all at the same time. I am still impressed at the dedication and professionalism he needed to make this sound fresh and spontaneous night after night for what was then still an indefinite run. It could so easily have become a static, routine performance this far into its course, but even though I knew Bruce would work hard not to let that happen, it was still remarkable how he could make you feel you were in a room full of people hearing him do this for the very first time. Part of this effect was created by what seems a genuinely thoughtful, often slow delivery, with quite long pauses in the middle of speech, as if he was formulating the words in front of you; totally convincing, even mesmerising. The lyrics were mostly faithful to the originals; occasionally a difference was apparent, such as 'rug mill' replacing 'textile mill' in 'My Hometown'.

The sound in the theatre was sparklingly clear and perfect, the acoustics so good that Bruce could step away from the microphones and address us a couple of times without any amplification. The lighting was simple but extremely effective; it changed so subtly you'd hardly notice. While singing about the desert, for example, the back of the stage had a sultry red glow like a sunrise or sunset. Bruce was often starkly silhouetted especially as a song draws to a close, fading to black before the next part. These elements made a huge contribution to the power of the experience.

Waves of emotion were balanced with absorbed listening to his narration and singing. Just seeing the man walk on stage brought the first swelling to my heart; thankfully the superb pacing and structure of the sequence was such that it wasn't constantly overwhelming. New Jersey was playfully described as 'Jerzekestan', as in a small country that no-one knows much about. He joked after 'My Father's House' that we were 'off suicide watch', recognising the need for some levity after the intensely personal parts. 'Tenth Avenue Freeze-Out' provided the emotional core to the middle section: a long, rambling meditation on the importance and power of the magic of the equation 1+1=3, love, music, the band, and of course the Big Man – Bruce cued a huge, long roaring crowd ovation, reminiscent of the audience response on recent tours. You'd have to be made of stone not to react to that; for me, I felt my heart bursting at such a moment of pure connection and unity with Bruce and everyone in that room. We know Bruce has so often reinvented – or more properly reverse-engineered - the arrangements of his music from band versions to acoustic performances. It struck me that there were many songs played which I'd never heard in person either on solo acoustic guitar, and particularly on solo piano. ('My Father's House' was an all-time first for me that night, finally completing my 'Nebraska' songs heard live after 36 years.) 'Born In The USA', remarkably, stood out for me even though I've heard him do several different acoustic versions over the years – it may be his most frequently changed song. Apart from the staggeringly intense, drawn-out blues slide guitar opening, I noticed that almost all of the rest – the vocal part of the song - was sung *a capella* (I think one of the only times I've heard Bruce sing a capella at any shows I attended was when he did 'Ain't Got You' on the *Tunnel* tour in 1988). Such an arrangement was even more effective than ever at stripping down the song to its essential element – the story of its lyrics, with really minimal guitar touches for the most part.

Midway through the night, Bruce took a two-song pause from his solo presentation by bringing on Patti Scialfa for a demonstration of how he hasn't been alone in this, either professionally or personally. Fittingly, the songs they performed together were 'Tougher Than The Rest' – done with him seated at the piano, and her standing nearby so they face each other, giving the impression of a song which connects them – and 'Brilliant Disguise', chosen to reflect on their life since the initial connection, with all the challenges and complications that come with the risk of trust.

The second part of the evening seemed to pass more rapidly, as it was dominated by the songs more than the stories which seem more prominent in the first section. True to form, Bruce drew the sequence to a close with the same immaculate sense of pacing he brings to any performance; letting one song flow into another was extremely effective to this end, such as the transition from 'Dancing In The Dark' into 'Land Of Hope And Dreams' (for once not introduced by its title) – the most intense and passionate performance I can remember of the latter, sung and played as if there was no tomorrow.

Nearly at the end, Bruce created a pause as if he was back from the 'main set' for an encore, with a final speech, reminding us again of his words in the book on how his promise, his magic trick, is not just about his story, but our story, him and us helping each other together, and united us all once again – following his recounting of his career as what he calls a 'long and noisy prayer' – with the recognition that he had come full circle from his childhood in a small town dominated by religion, to a point where (always the Catholic) he was once again 'surrounded by God'. What more fitting conclusion to that 'prayer' than the universal one, the Lord's Prayer, which seemed perfectly appropriate in this context, regardless of anyone's creed or beliefs. Only one song could follow that, and that's what 'Born To Run' did, an anthem brought home to its elemental centre, the quest for love. You want to know if love is real? There it was, flowing both ways. The lights went up, Patti re-joined Bruce for a minute or so while they took their final bows together, amid a frenzy of audience camera activity after the strict photographic ban during the show; she walked off, and after a few handshakes with some at the front, Bruce walked off too, and it was over.

As the arc of the stories and songs covering Bruce's career completed, there was an unmistakable sense that this was a summary (logically complementing and following on from the autobiography), and like the familiar idea that at the end of things one gets the impression of your life flashing before you – as a long-time fan since 1976, I certainly had the effect of my 'past Bruce life' encompassed in these two-and-something hours. I know others felt the same, and potentially of course it's a distressing idea to think that something so special and essential has to come to an end sometime... but right now, the story – our combined story - goes on. I never see any point in speculating 'is this the last time?'; far better to focus on making the most of however long this continues. But while the inevitable awaits us all, as Bruce himself often ponders on our mortality, this was another (and a unique one) in a long line of gifts he's given us, a celebration of life, love, faith, hope, dreams, and reality; all the things that make existence precious and life worth living. I have seen Bruce many, many times, and marvel at how after all this time he has brought us something breathtakingly new and vital out of a collection of – on the face of it - old songs and stories. It was a magnificent feat, and for an old fan like me it felt like a baptism, a renewal, sending me forth to face life with new courage and resolve, living the shared story with my friends and loved ones, looking forward to our next rendezvous further on up the road. Yet again, I have been so fortunate, and am highly conscious of dear friends who would have loved to make it, but for whatever reason couldn't. I hoped that as many fans as possible got the chance to do this too. I have seen the past of rock'n'roll, and its name is Bruce Springsteen – on Broadway.

International friends on Broadway

*Brother Jim's picture**

*My gratitude and sympathy to Jim, who bought our tickets but was then unable to join me on the trip. I carried a picture of him with me to the show in his honour.

RIP Holly: this was the last time I saw Holly Cara Price, who didn't come to the show but helped coordinate and joined a big group of international friends for a pizza dinner that day. #MTG

2023-2025

The *2023-2025 International* tour

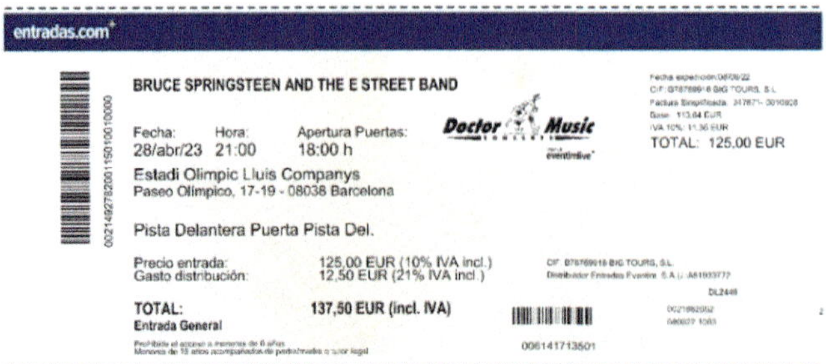
entradas.com

BRUCE SPRINGSTEEN AND THE E STREET BAND

Fecha: 28/abr/23 Hora: 21:00 Apertura Puertas: 18:00 h

Estadi Olimpic Lluis Companys
Paseo Olimpico, 17-19 - 08038 Barcelona

Pista Delantera Puerta Pista Del.

Precio entrada: 125,00 EUR (10% IVA incl.)
Gasto distribución: 12,50 EUR (21% IVA incl.)

TOTAL: 137,50 EUR (incl. IVA)
Entrada General

TOTAL: 125,00 EUR

006141713501

28 April 2023: Barcelona, Estadi Olímpic Lluís Companys

Mike's birthday fell between the two Barcelona shows starting the 2023 European leg, so it felt rude not to go, and Deirdre joined our apartment crew. Pre-show, we met local friend Salvador to see an outdoor photo exhibition by Francesc Fabregas he'd helped with. There was a single line for both GA and pit entry, which meant a long wait to get into the stadium, having traipsed all around the complex. By the time we got to the pit the back was busy, so we settled at the right side instead – a good spot to meet many friends, including Danny, Sergio, Malcolm, Paul, Beverly, Laurie, Roger and Winni. As the night darkened, new stage lighting features were noticeable. After multiple soundcheck takes, 'Human Touch' was a tour debut, and 'Glory Days' featured a rare appearance by Patti, along with guests Michelle Obama and Kate Capshaw. Thanks to Ekaterina for my ticket! We dedicated the trip to our dear departed friend Judith (RIP).

Sal photo by Kate

entradas.com
BRUCE SPRINGSTEEN AND THE E STREET BAND
Fecha: Hora: Apertura Puertas:
30/abr/23 21:00 18:00 h
Estadi Olimpic Lluis Companys
Paseo Olímpico, 17-19 - 08038 Barcelona
Pista Delantera Puerta Pista Del.
Precio entrada: 125,00 EUR (10% IVA incl.)
Gasto distribución: 12,50 EUR (21% IVA incl.)
TOTAL: 137,50 EUR (incl. IVA)
Entrada General
TOTAL: 125,00 EUR
006150311901

30 April 2023: Barcelona, Estadi Olímpic Lluís Companys

After a deceptive weather forecast, Mike, Deirdre and I had not long joined the long, slow entry line for the second show (barcode reader problems both nights) when the heavens opened and we got thoroughly soaked to the skin, caught out without waterproof clothing. After a couple of hours, not only waterlogged but also chilled by a mountain breeze, Mike and I were almost ready to give up and go home, but having made it to our side pit spot again, we stuck it out – I spent most of the show shivering and shaking, convinced I was catching pneumonia. Monika, Suso, José, Phil & Cinzia came to say Hi, as did Caroline & Ralph: Caroline got her birthday wish with the opener 'My Love Will Not Let You Down'. 'Trapped', 'Johnny 99' and 'Ramrod' were set variations. Both nights, for 'Letter To You', 'Last Man Standing' and 'I'll See You In My Dreams', the words were added to the screen in Catalan. Both Jon Landau and Thom Zimny were seen in the pit. Heading back, my Metro ticket had disintegrated into mush in the rain – thankfully Ekaterina translated and saved the day!

30 May 2023: Edinburgh, BT Murrayfield Stadium

A month after Barcelona, I headed to Edinburgh for the first E Street Band show there since 1981, and Bruce's first time at the Murrayfield stadium. I'd won a pair of extra seated PDF tickets (above) which I donated, but kept no image of my own animated mobile barcode ticket, the trend for concert tickets these days. Jake briefly draped a Scottish Saltire flag over his shoulders. A rare chance to see the fab Donna from Bruce Funds in the pit, and a special family gathering for my host Big Neil with both his sons Callum and Jamie there together.

Neil, Helen and me at the back of the pit, Murrayfield 2023
Photo thanks to Scottish Rugby

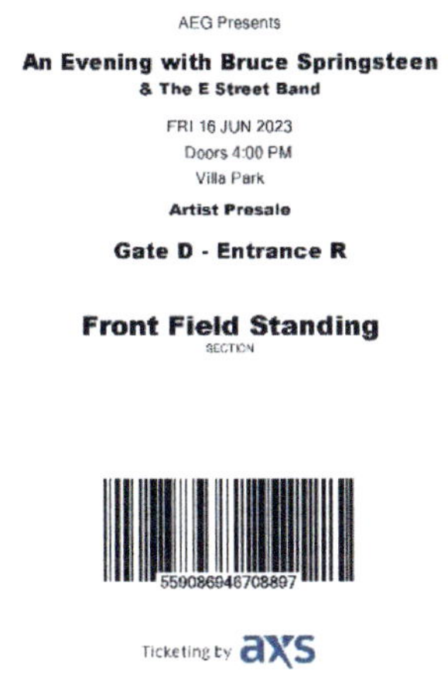

16 June 2023: Birmingham, Villa Park

A delight to have Tanya with me for my return to Villa Park, the first time since 1988 – and the Midlands stadium didn't seem to have changed much. 'My Hometown' and 'The River' (a tour premiere) were the main changes on this date. A large and incredibly drunk family in front of us in the pit, boozing non-stop, unsurprisingly got on Tanya's nerves and she moved elsewhere for a while, having earlier been pestered by another drunk guy. I snapped the band line-up, coincidentally highlighting the four veterans Max, Stevie, Roy and Garry on the big screen also – the 'Mount Rushmore' of E Street. What a treat to spot old friend 'Doctor' Tony nearby, still able to fit into his 1985 custom-made 'Dr Zoom & The Sonic Boom' t-shirt! Lovely chats with Julie, Anita and Paul too – also welcome during the long wait queuing for the local train back into Birmingham afterwards.

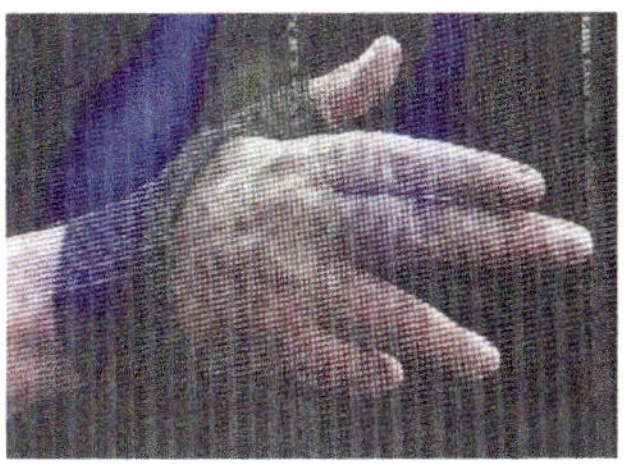

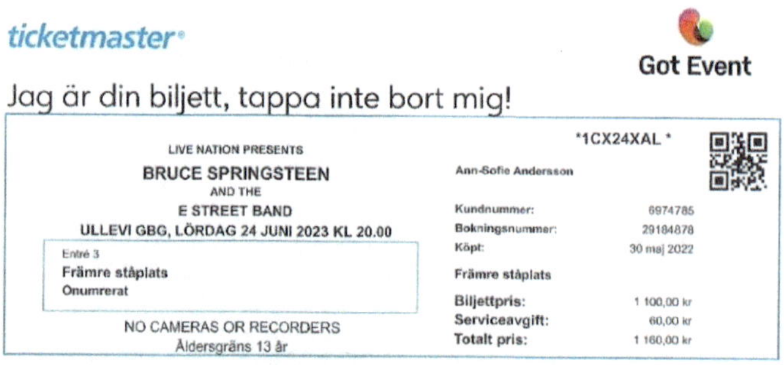

ticketmaster®

Got Event

Jag är din biljett, tappa inte bort mig!

LIVE NATION PRESENTS
BRUCE SPRINGSTEEN
AND THE
E STREET BAND
ULLEVI GBG, LÖRDAG 24 JUNI 2023 KL 20.00

Entré 3
Främre ståplats
Onumrerat

NO CAMERAS OR RECORDERS
Åldersgräns 13 år

1CX24XAL

Ann-Sofie Andersson

Kundnummer:	6974785
Bokningsnummer:	29184878
Köpt:	30 maj 2022
Främre ståplats	
Biljettpris:	1 100,00 kr
Serviceavgift:	60,00 kr
Totalt pris:	1 160,00 kr

24 June 2023: Gothenburg, Ullevi

'We're all in the same boat!' Three midsummer shows at Gothenburg had to be done, and when Ralf tipped us off to a bargain boat hotel in the harbour, a bunch of us became the Shipmates; an ideal base to stagger home to after the concerts, once including our own private live acoustic session, thanks to Jonathan & Anneli. Gothenburg is a social magnet, and we met so many special people over the week – much-missed dear folks like Connor (for the last time – RIP bro), Salla and Ellinor; and new friends like the fabulous Nicki, who joined us to hang out in the pit each night, and held a magical book signing event (thanks to host Anders) which also attracted some E Streeters straight off another boat: Curtis, Anthony, Lisa, Ozzie, and Garry, plus non-stop photographer Rob (Pam Springsteen was also in town and taking pictures). 'Tack' to Annsofie for my ticket.

Rarities for the first night were 'The Ties That Bind', 'Lucky Town' and 'Land Of Hope And Dreams'. Swedish subtitles appeared on the big screen for key songs on each date.

Gothenburg gatherings with fab folks, Geezers and Shipmates

ticketmaster

Got Event

Keep me safe, I'm your ticket

LIVE NATION PRESENTS
BRUCE SPRINGSTEEN
AND
THE E STREET BAND
ULLEVI GBG, MÅNDAG 26 JUNI 2023 KL 20.00

Entré 3
Främre ståplats
Onumrerat

NO CAMERAS OR RECORDERS
Åldersgräns 13 år

"J51M5YF-D"

Edvard Sønderland

Customer number:	8338012
Order number:	29190128
Purchased:	30 maj 2022
Främre ståplats	
Ticket price:	1 100,00 kr
Service fee:	60,00 kr
Total price:	1 160,00 kr

26 June 2023: Gothenburg, Ullevi

'Better Days' was soundchecked but not played for night two; however, a classic that had been rehearsed (multiple request signs were coordinated in the pit at the first show) - 'Racing In The Street' – made its tour premiere, and marked the key central place, both in the set and overall in the stand. Thanks to Edvard for the ticket.

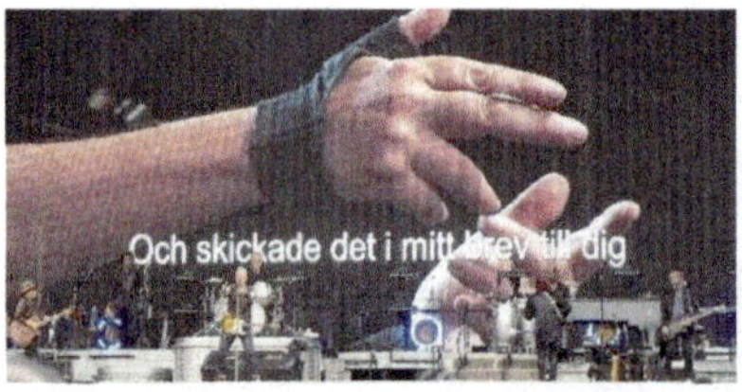

Goodnight, Gothenburg!

ticketmaster
Got Event
Keep me safe, I'm your ticket

LIVE NATION PRESENTS
BRUCE SPRINGSTEEN
AND
THE E STREET BAND
ULLEVI GBG, ONSDAG 28 JUNI 2023 KL 20.00

Entré 3
Främre ståplats
Onumrerat

NO CAMERAS OR RECORDERS
Åldersgräns 13 år

-$9 4JB8U
Saoirse Houston
Customer number: 8343375
Order number: 29212573
Purchased: 30 maj 2022
Främre ståplats
Ticket price: 1 100,00 kr
Service fee: 60,00 kr
Total price: 1 160,00 kr

28 June 2023: Gothenburg, Ullevi

'It's time to break the stadium' read one large fan request sign, and after the treat of a rare opening 'Night' in its European debut for the tour, the final full-band song for Gothenburg was indeed the famous stadium breaker, and a few of us had our 'wrecking crew' t-shirts ready for it as well. Thanks to Saoirse for my ticket.

After the last song. 'I'll See You In My Dreams', Bruce promised 'We will be back!' Whether there'll actually be a return to Gothenburg itself, only time will tell; but 2024 certainly brought another visit to Sweden, in Stockholm.

Appropriately for Sweden, my Stockholm friend Ellinor, who'd had to miss the other two shows for health reasons, managed to make it across country in time for the final date, and after a joyful rendezvous with Jim and me, she lit up the pit with her infectious enthusiasm. Go Ellinor!

'We will be back!'

Photo thanks to Ellinor

6 July 2023: London, Hyde Park

Bruce and the E Street Band (recently oddly abbreviated to 'Springsteen E Street Band' in so many official listings) played two outdoor dates in London in July 2023, both headlining the BST Hyde Park festival, with support acts: The Chicks and Frank Turner & The Sleeping Souls. Trying to minimise my time inside the venue, it took much tricky triangulation to meet up with my main crew of friends installed part-way back in the main GA area. Nice to see Rod there too, although we almost missed each other in the crowd. Deirdre and I had a chat with Mark Rashotte, there to see Jake. Looking at the Carlton Tower hotel nearby, I thought how far Bruce had come since he stayed there in 1981. We both decided to head out beyond the fence for the encores, where Mike and Dave were enjoying a free show with a limited view but more comfort.

Hyde Park view of the Carlton Tower hotel, Bruce's 1981 base

Receipt
Order #3474687
Date of issue: 18 July 2022, 12:28 (GMT)

festicket

This is not your ticket! You will receive your ticket(s) separately.

Your Package

- 2 x Bruce Springsteen | Primary Entry - Saturday | Payment Plan to **American Express presents BST Hyde Park 2023** (8 July 2023 14:00-23:00)

8 July 2023: London, Hyde Park

The second day at the BST Hyde Park festival featured support acts The Chicks again, plus James Bay, and Brittney Spencer. Having enjoyed the 'outside experience' at the end of the previous show, and with little energy on my third trip into London in three days (Badlands hosted an excellent book signing event with Nicki Germaine on 7 July), I opted to join Mike and other friends like Annie, Colin, Sharon, Jeremy and Debs outside the perimeter fence again for a relaxing free picnic with shelter from trees, convenient conveniences and excellent sound. They always open up the gates around encore time too, meaning a strategic position affords a clear view of the stage later. After Mike pioneered this cunning plan awhile before, it's definitely our preferred idea for any future BST events – and saves a small fortune, too. Mike's commission is also very reasonable by comparison.

The 'outside experience' at Hyde Park

5 May 2024: Cardiff, Principality Stadium

Bruce's first European show after postponing many 2023 dates due to illness, a welcome return indoors to the closed-roofed Welsh stadium, as was a rare (setlisted) 'So Young And In Love', its third ever appearance in Europe and a first for me. 'Better Days' was a sign request. With at least two signs for 'If I Was The Priest', Bruce finally gave it a European premiere. Lovely to hang out with Ekaterina & Tanya, and to see Nicki, Annsofie & Jennifer, Ellie & H, 'Matey', Ramona and Peter & Margaret among others. Sorry to miss Paul there!

Polaroid by Kate

Welsh Druids? and Peter – photo by Margaret

22 May 2024: Sunderland, Stadium Of Light

One of the wettest shows, with almost non-stop heavy rain all day; Jim and I delayed going out for our spot in the pit with Dave & Debs, but still got soaked. The band fared no better, with puddles frequently being swept off the stage. Bruce optimistically started with 'Waitin' On A Sunny Day', but it was going to be quite a wait. 'Racing In The Street' was a blissful interlude when we could briefly forget the discomfort. Bruce danced in the puddles, and almost stripped all his top layers off but kept a white top on – unfortunately not enough protection to stop him having to postpone the next few shows due to illness; and unwittingly leading to the unplanned 2025 European leg by doing so, expanding on the make-up dates.

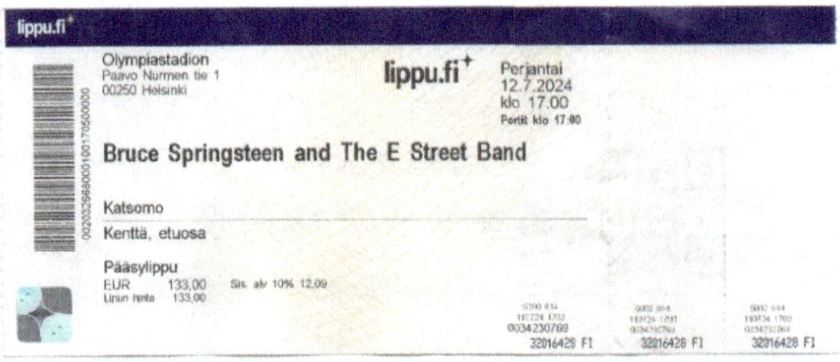

12 July 2024: Helsinki, Olympiastadion

Retired rock'n'roll tourists: Mike was meant to travel with me to join Dave in Finland, but was unwell and caught us up in Sweden later instead. Returning to the Olympiastadion, site of the longest ever show, Bruce rehearsed some interesting choices in the soundcheck, including 'Long Walk Home', 'Into The Fire' and (appropriately for the local fan club) 'This Hard Land'. 'Long Walk Home' was played and was a tour premiere, the first band rendition since 2014, and Bruce admitted they hadn't played it in a while. Given the ominous state of US politics, it became a regular rallying call at most remaining 2024 concerts. While song requests continued to feature on signs, for those up close there was also a newer trend for requests (sometimes suggesting trades) for harmonicas from Bruce. Finnish subtitles appeared on the screen during 'Letter To You', 'Last Man Standing' and 'I'll See You In My Dreams'. Noting the long Nordic summer evening light, during 'Twist And Shout' while Bruce was debating with Stevie about going home, he admitted: 'It sorta is still daytime, I guess! But that's a trick up here, I know that!'

15 July 2024: Stockholm, Strawberry Arena

Lovely to catch up with local friend Ellinor again, who unfortunately couldn't make it to a show this time. The tickets stated 'Friends Arena', but the huge 65,000 capacity venue (with a closed roof for concerts, where Bruce played in 2013) had just changed its name to 'Strawberry Arena'. After the recent news of an attempted assassination of Trump, Bruce played 'Into The Fire' and 'Land Of Hope And Dreams', adding an ongoing introduction to 'Long Walk Home': 'This is a prayer for my country.'

The 'Retired Rock'n'Roll Tourists' with Mukul, Tim & Ruth

18 July 2024: Stockholm, Strawberry Arena

We bumped into Nicki on the street, who held a book signing event hosted by Anders again. Mike took the best photo of the trip with us reflected in her shades. Playing indoors meant the band could slip on in the dark and have a very dramatic opening with the stage lights coming on suddenly both nights – 'Seeds' opened this time. 'I'm On Fire' was a spontaneous audible, one of nine changes to the previous setlist.

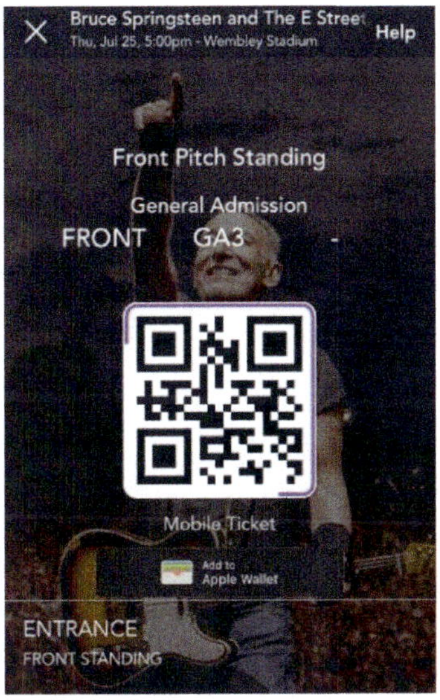

25 July 2024: London, Wembley Stadium

Outdoors again for the two London shows, luckily only slightly rainy for the first night at Wembley Stadium. Being the capital and the finale for the 2024 European leg, lots of friends were in town for both shows. A special treat to see John, Tom & Laura there together – Laura's first Bruce show, too. On the 26th, Badlands hosted a book event with Nicki, and that evening Thom Zimny presented a 'Springsteen On Screen' collection of film clips at the Prince Charles Cinema.

Dave's 'Tourists' designs

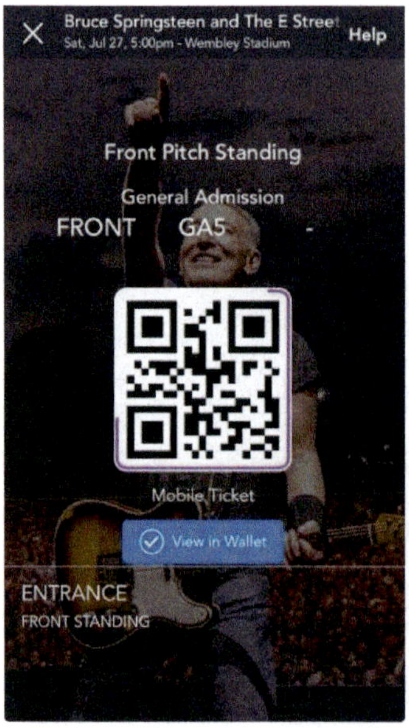

27 July 2024: London, Wembley Stadium

'Connor's Corner', our part of the back of the pit, was filled with many friends together again for the last night. Bruce soundchecked 'Tougher Than The Rest', 'Death To My Hometown' and 'Mary's Place', and played all three among nine different songs from the first show. Patti made a rare appearance on 'Tougher Than The Rest', with an amusing moment when her top got tangled in Bruce's guitar, and they had to separate themselves.

Next up would be the 'bonus' spring 2025 European leg. Bruce's Sunderland antics in the rain meant four continental shows postponed, the basis for several weeks of extra dates and a third year for the '2023-2025 International' tour.

TO BE CONTINUED ...

In summer 2025, after the five UK shows in Manchester and Liverpool take place, there will be an online update with notes from those shows at this link:

https://docs.google.com/document/d/1FYxYuHdtnvsT2NG121D83X83vtm-sVcl/edit

Or just scan the QR code below with your phone camera:

ESSENTIAL REFERENCE SITES:

I can't recommend **Brucebase** enough, beyond saying it's an indispensable and highly accurate resource for any Springsteen fan. The range of reference options in its Site Navigation panel is superb. A co-operative and comprehensive project, it well deserves its own description 'the most complete guide to the music of Bruce Springsteen available on the internet today':
http://brucebase.wikidot.com

You can subscribe to Ken Rosen's *Kingdom Of Days* series for daily history emails, and find other well-researched postings at his **E Street Shuffle** blog:
https://estreetshuffle.com

The **Bruce Springsteen Archives and Center for American Music** has its own site and social media:
https://springsteenarchives.org

Eddy Wehbe's excellent **Springsteen Lyrics** site is superb for details of Bruce's lyrics, official and unofficial releases – it also provides news updates:
http://springsteenlyrics.com

Linda Rottiers' remarkable site **Covered By Springsteen** does what its name describes, providing an exhaustive resource on songs by other artists which Bruce has covered:
https://www.coveredbybrucespringsteen.com

Jay Lustig's **NJ Arts** site has excellent and comprehensive NJ news coverage, and you can subscribe to his newsletter for updates:
https://www.njarts.net

MORE LINKS FOR BRUCE FANS:

https://brucefunds.org/home

"Since the Wrecking Ball tour in 2012, **Bruce Funds** has helped nearly 2,000 fans around the world. If the spirit of what I do exists in you too, then you can gift your tickets yourself wherever you are." – Donna, Bruce Funds Founder

---

https://badlands.co.uk/pages/bruce-springsteen

"**Badlands** has been specialising in all things Bruce Springsteen since 1985. Whether you're a lifelong fan or new to his electrifying world we've got everything you need to fuel your Springsteen obsession."

https://creators.spotify.com/pod/show/jeff-matthews4

If you love Bruce Springsteen's music, **The E Street Café Podcast** is for you, covering news, topical debate about Bruce and more happening on E Street. Look out for special guest conversations and a lot of fun along the way!

POINT BLANK

a Wild and Innocent production

The original Wild and Innocent Productions companion site continues as long as Google Sites permit:
https://sites.google.com/site/wildandinnocentproductions/

The Wild and Innocent Productions download site, offering free PDFs of the original publications and other archives, continues at MEGA:
https://mega.nz/fm/1D4AWYjQ

ALSO FROM TRETHEWEY PRESS

Trethewey Press: The Collected Poetry of Joy French

2024

Amazon paperback and eBook
Scan QR code below to order

In memory of my dear mother Joy (1921-2007). This compilation of her verses particularly captures and summarises my impression of her life in Devon during the 1990s, the first decade she and my father Arthur spent there after retirement to the West country. All proceeds go to the Afrinspire charity.

Ipplepen by Arthur French

2024

A historical guide to the village of Ipplepen, Devon, first published in 2003

Arthur French (1920-2016):

'I first came to Ipplepen in 1948. My father-in-law, who had a shop in Warland, Totnes, brought me here because in Ipplepen and Torbryan, he said, they made the best local cider.'

With permission from Arthur's original publisher and illustrator, Obelisk Publications, this new 2024 reprint seeks to preserve his work for the future; as he says in the book, 'history matters today'.

DAN FRENCH became a Springsteen fan in the late 1970s, and since first going to see him in concert in 1981 has travelled around the UK, Europe, to the United States and once to Australia – often with the excuse of doing international ice cream research – for many more shows, averaging about 5 per year over 44 years so far in 2025.

In the 1980s he published the UK fanzine Point Blank and other independent fan productions, later running several Bruce- and music-related Facebook groups, and more recently contributing to The E Street Café Podcast.

He lives at Signal Hill, his flat in Hertfordshire with its nearby Overground Garage (Little Stevenage), surrounded by too much Springsteen memorabilia, too little space, and maybe just enough ice cream.

TRETHEWEY

9 781738 574353

Printed in Great Britain
by Amazon

61075730R00179